Canadian National

CANADIAN NATIONAL

Edited by
Keith MacKenzie

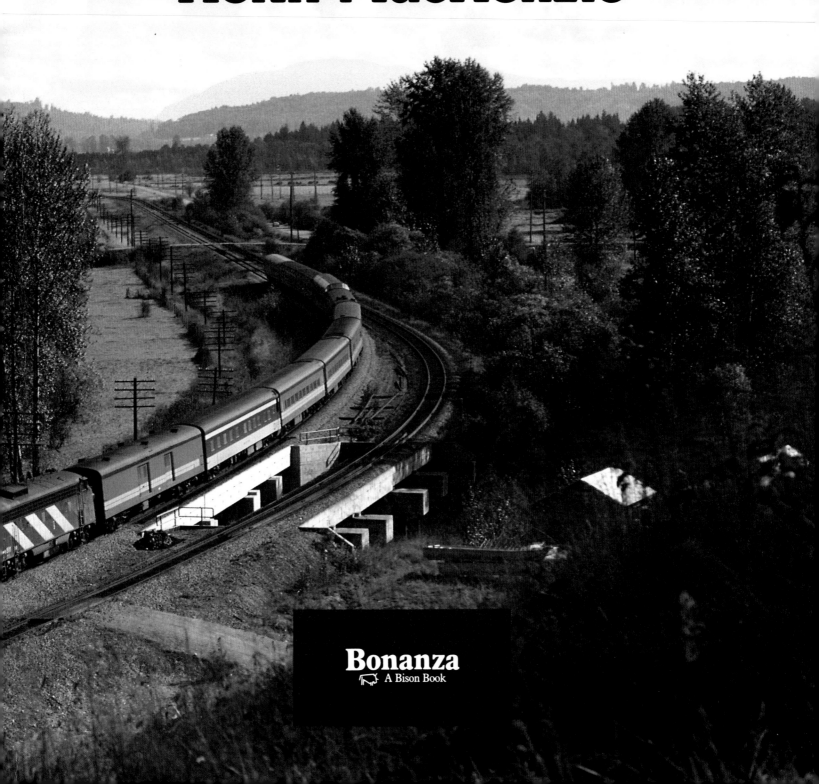

Bonanza
A Bison Book

Published 1988 by
Bonanza Books, distributed by
Crown Publishers Inc

Produced by Bison Books Corp
15 Sherwood Place
Greenwich, CT 06830, USA

Printed in Hong Kong

ISBN 0-517-65854-2
h g f e d c b a

Picture Credits

All photographs courtesy of CN except:
Burlington Northern Railroad: 88 (top left)
Canadian Pacific Railroad: 28–29 (bottom), 29 (top), 30, 31, 32–33, 34, 35, 52
Grand Trunk Western: 14–15 (bottom), 15 (top), 16–17, 18–19, 21, 42–43, 44–45 (right), 50–51, 55, 55–57 (all), 58–59, 90, 95 (bottom right)
Nils Huxtable/Steamscenes: 1, 2–3, 60–61 (left), 72–73
Marine Atlantic: 121 (bottom), 122–123
Tourism Office, City of Toronto: 124
VIA Rail Canada: 86 (top and bottom), 87 (top and bottom), 88 (bottom left)

Designed by Tom Debolski
Captioned by Timothy Jacobs

Page 1: Canadian National's vintage number 1392 seems to smile a fateful smile across the years—from the age of steam to today, when diesels hold sway.
Pages 2-3: A Canadian National diesel passenger train speeds along under gorgeous Canadian skies, in the days before VIA Rail took over all such Canadian passenger service.
These pages: A long CN triple header pulls out of the loading facility at the Cardinal River Coal Mine at Luscar, Alberta.

Contents

The Early Years

The First Railway in Canada

In the early 19th century, British North America was very different from today's Canada. There were fewer than two million settlers in a land of almost ten million square kilometres of dense forests, vast swamps, and spectacular mountain ranges. The established colonies were Nova Scotia, Prince Edward Island, New Brunswick, Newfoundland, Lower Canada, and Upper Canada. Between the latter and the great mountain ranges far to the west lay Prince Rupert's Land, owned by the Hudson's Bay Company. This fur-trading company also controlled the coastal strip beyond the mountains, but there were few settlers there.

Life was challenging. Long winters brought bitter cold and blizzards. Narrow dirt roads linking settlements often had stumps sticking up right in the middle of them, and countless potholes. Rain and spring thaws turned them into impassable quagmires, so that travellers—whether on foot, horseback, in wagons or stagecoaches—sometimes had to wait several days for a road to dry before they could go on.

Rivers and lakes served as main thoroughfares, the highways of the nation. Halifax, Quebec City, and Saint John, New Brunswick were the most important ports, bustling with people and activity. Ships from Europe and the United States could sail 800 kilometres up the St Lawrence River to Montreal. They carried linens, chinaware, fashionable clothes, machinery, and many other goods needed by settlers scattered across a young country. But Montreal was as far as ships could go, because of the Lachine Rapids.

Above the rapids, boats carried passengers and freight between cities and towns on the Great Lakes. There also was a chain of rivers and lakes leading westward from Montreal which made it possible for men using canoes—long, wide ones, each big enough to hold 10 or 12 persons with cargo and supplies—to reach the Prairies and beyond.

Yet travel by water also posed problems. For five or six months a year, ice prevented travel and business slowed down while people waited for the spring break-up. In summer, rapids and waterfalls caused many difficulties and delays, so in some places canals were built to bypass them. They helped but, because there were many locks and they were small, travel was slow. Still, where there were no canals, people had to unload their goods from ships or canoes, and either carry both their goods and their boats or use wagons or carts along primitive roads.

Businessmen in Upper and Lower Canada and the Maritimes knew that for their trade to prosper and the country to develop, faster and better ways of moving people and goods would have to be found. They were very excited, therefore, when in the mid-1820s railways using steam-powered locomotives appeared, first in England and later in the United States.

By 1832, a group of Montreal businessmen called 'The Company of Proprietors' began planning Canada's first railway. The Champlain and St Lawrence Railroad opened for business on 21 July 1836 with a celebration attended by hundreds of people. Among those who took the first train ride in Canada were the Governor General of Lower Canada Lord Gosford, and French Canadian 'patriote' Louis-Joseph Papineau.

Below left: This artist's rendition of Canada's first locomotive, the *Dorchester*, depicts the locomotive's maiden run on 21 July 1836. Note the similarity between this loco and its prototype, the Stephenson *Rocket (above)*. Early locos were skitterish, but proved a point.

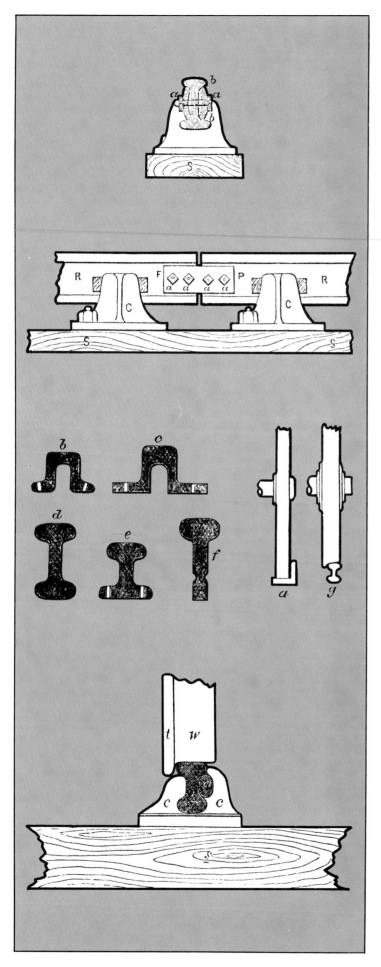

Early railroad inventors went wild with rail designs, and early Canadian railroads used nearly all such designs—some of which are depicted *above*. The brouhaha ended when the American Robert Stevens invented his 'inverted T' rail. *Opposite:* An early express engine, which bears design similarities to the *Dorchester*, but on a larger scale.

The line was 14 miles long, and ran between La Prairie on the St Lawrence River near Montreal and Saint-Jean (then St Johns) on the Richelieu. It was built to replace a road which served as the northernmost link in the traffic route between Montreal and New York City, and which had itself been built to circumvent rapids in the Richelieu which prevented boats from sailing between the St Lawrence and Lake Champlain.

The Champlain and St Lawrence Railroad was a big success. Its little locomotive regularly ran its trackage in less than an hour, reaching the amazing speed of 30 mph. Even in good weather, it took a stagecoach three hours to cover the same distance by road.

Because everyone wanted to use 'the iron horse,' a steady flow of passengers and freight soon made the line profitable.

Early railways were quite different from those of today. Their tracks were of wood, with long strips of iron spiked along the tops. Because heat and cold made the iron expand and contract, the strips often came loose and curled up at the ends. When a train passed over such 'snake rails,' as they were called, the ends tore the undersides of the coaches, and made holes in water tanks behind locomotives.

The first locomotive used in Canada, the *Dorchester*, was imported from England. It was 13 feet long and, like almost all early locomotives, burned wood to make the steam which powered it. (Today's locomotives are about 90 feet long and use diesel fuel to generate the electricity which runs them.) The *Dorchester* also had a very tall smokestack, to prevent large sparks from flying into the air and setting fire to trees and grass beside the tracks.

Railway journeys could be like carnival rides. For example, at the opening of the Montreal and Lachine, another early railway, the Scottish engineer was so proud of his Scottish-built locomotive that he pulled the coaches filled with very important passengers at 60mph. Not only were they terrified, but the bumping and jolting squashed many expensive top hats and hoop skirts, and sparks shooting from the smokestack burned large holes in ladies' dresses. The engineer very nearly lost his job on the first day!

Railways changed the lives of many Canadian settlers. Before there were trains, earning money wasn't easy for people in rural areas. But railways paid local men to lay tracks and once a line was opened farmers could use trains to ship their produce for sale far from home. Eggs, butter, milk, fruit, chickens, rabbits—all were sent off to city markets, and dollars came back. What's more, farmers were paid to provide wood for locomotives, and while a train was stopped, local craftsmen had a chance to sell their wares to passengers.

Thus a new rail line always meant prosperity and growth. In fact, more than one small town actually moved to a new location to be closer to where the trains ran. The arrival of the train was the highlight of a day. A crowd would wait at the station to stare at wealthy travellers and chat with passengers who got off to take a stroll.

Railways also built telegraph lines to send messages from one station to another, warning their workers of problems along the line or informing them of train movements. Naturally, the telegraph began to provide services to communitities as well. In emergencies, its operator could wire for help, and important news arrived much faster by wire than by mail. Trains also provided the means for people in small places to feel closer to the rest of the world, as they brought newpapers and letters in a few days rather than in weeks or months as stagecoaches had done.

Government Help for Railways

In 1841 the British Parliament, on a recommendation by Lord Durham, joined Lower and Upper Canada into one Province of Canada. The need to tie the new province together with rails was making itself felt. But making money in the railway business in Canada was not easy to do. By 1850, although about 40 companies had been granted permission by the government to build rail lines, only six, including the Champlain and St Lawrence, had actually laid track. Of the six railways that did lay track, three were short lines bypassing obstructions in water routes: the Champlain and St Lawrence; the Montreal and Lachine Railroad, 8 miles long, skirting the Lachine Rapids in the St Lawrence River; and the Erie and Ontario Railway, 11 miles long, built to bypass the Niagra Falls. There were 80 miles in all.

The problem was a lack of investment capital. Before any money could be earned, much had to be spent on surveying routes, clearing and levelling land, determining how best to cross streams and swamps, laying rail, and then importing locomotives and passenger and freight cars from England or the United States.

Businessmen in the young colonies simply were not wealthy enough to provide the necessary funds. Investors elsewhere were reluctant to put money into a railway in British North America because they thought the population was too small to make it pay.

By the end of the 1840s British North America was realizing both the need for railway expansion and the difficulty of financing it. British and American contractors discovered the virgin field awaiting them. The example set in the United States was powerful. Massachusetts had guaranteed bonds of local roads to the extent of $8 million, and though New York's experience had been more

varied, the successes were stressed and the failures were plausibly explained away.

It was clear that, if Canada was ever to have a reliable rail network, the government would have to help companies find money to pay for building it. Francis Hincks, merchant, journalist, and politician, moderate reformer, and Canada's first notable finance minister, took the initiative. As inspector-general in the second Baldwin-La-Fontaine cabinet, he brought down the first installment of his railway policy in 1849. He had drawn up two memoranda—one suggesting that the crown lands in the province might be offered as security for the capital to build the road within the province, and the other urging the Imperial government to undertake the road from Halifax to Quebec. Financiers gave no encouragement to the first suggestion, and the British government had not replied to the second by the end of the session of 1848–49. Accordingly, in April 1849 Hincks brought down a new policy, based upon a suggestion of the directors of the St Lawrence & Atlantic. The proposal, called the Guarantee Act of 1849, was to guarantee the interest, not exceeding 6 percent, on half the bonds of any railway over 75 miles long, and whenever half the road had been constructed the province was to be protected by a first charge after the bondholders' lien.

Even with this aid construction did not proceed swiftly. It was still necessary for the companies to complete half the road before qualifying for government assistance. This the St Lawrence road effected slowly, in face of quarrels with contractors, repudiation of calls by shareholders, and hesitancy of banks to make advances. The Great Western did not get underway until 1851, when American finan-

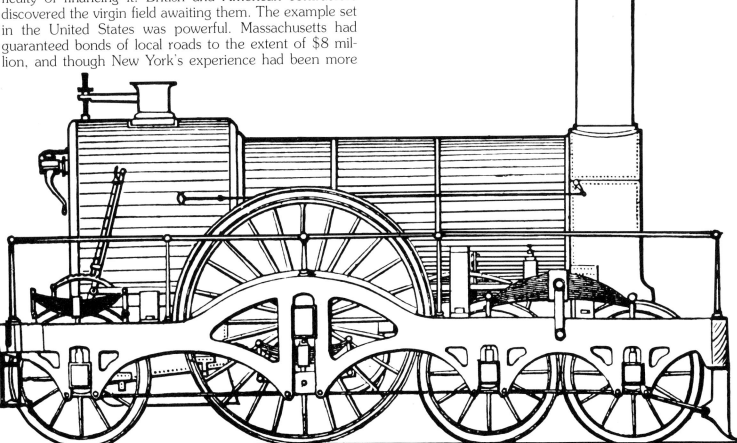

These pages: The Grand Trunk Railway's St Williams, Ontario station is shown here on a fine 19th century day. In evidence are baggage facilities (left end of building), express and telegraph service signs, train schedule (the chalkboard above the seated man in the bowler hat) and gentlemen and ladies in all their travelling finery.

ciers connected with the New York Central took shares and a place on the directorate. In the same year the Toronto, Simcoe & Huron, later known as the Northern, began construction.

Not surprisingly, many new lines were now begun. In fact during the next 65 years some 34,915 miles of track were laid between the Atlantic and the Pacific Oceans, uniting a new nation. Especially between 1850 and 1860, many small lines were built to link groups of neighbouring towns, and longer, more expensive networks were developed to connect major centers.

The 8 or 10 years which followed 1849 are notable not only for a sudden outburst of railway construction and speculative activity throughout the provinces, but for the beginning of that close connection between politics and railways which is distinctively Canadian. In this era parliament became the field of railway debate. Local politicians discovered the cash value of votes and influence. Statesmen began to talk of links of Empire and began to press the claims of their constituencies for needed railway communications. Cabinets realized the value of the charters they could grant or the credit they could pledge, and contractors swarmed to the task.

In the Maritimes

Meanwhile, suggestions from the Maritime Provinces had brought still more ambitious schemes within practical range. These led Hincks to take the second step in his policy of aid to railways.

In the Maritime colonies, starting railways was more difficult. From 1835 to 1850, many railways had been projected, but, with the exception of a small coal tramway in Nova Scotia, built in 1839 from the Albion coal mines to tidewater, not a mile was built before 1847. As early as 1827 there were plans to build a line from St Andrews on the Bay of Fundy to Quebec City. In 1835 a railway association was formed in St Andrews, an exploratory survey was made and the interest of lower Canada was enlisted. In the following year New Brunswick gave a charter to the St Andrews & Quebec Railroad, and the Imperial government agreed to bear the cost of a survey, but it was speedily halted because of protests from Maine. There was no clear border between the future New Brunswick and the United States, and the American Government protested that the line would run through what they claimed was part of the United States, so to avoid bad feelings the British Government abandoned the railway project. In 1842 the Ashburton Treaty assigned to the United States a great part of the territory through which the line was projected, and the promoters gave up.

In 1845 the railway mania in England brought a revival of all colonial schemes. Sir Richard Broun took up the plan for a line from Halifax to Quebec. This discussion revived the flagging hopes of St Andrews, and a beginning was made by a railway from St Andrews to Woodstock, the New Brunswick & Canada, for which ground was broken in November 1847. In 1853, a company was formed to build another long line, this time between Portland in Maine, and Halifax. However, after only a few miles of track had been laid the company ran out of money.

The provincial legislature concluded early that it would be impossible to induce private interests to build an intercolonial road unaided. They were unanimous also, not yet having emerged from colonial dependence, in wanting to throw the greater burden of such aid on the British government. In the absence of a colonial federation the United Kingdom was the main connecting link between the colonies in British North America and was presumably most interested in matters affecting more than a single colony. The British government, however, had by this time decided that the old policy of treating the colonies as an estate or plantation of the mother country, protecting or developing them in return for the monopoly of their trade, did not pay. It had reluctantly conceded them political home rule; it was soon to thrust upon them freedom of trade; and it was not inclined to retain burdens when it had given up privileges. Mr Gladstone, secretary for the Colonies, agreed, however, in 1846, to have a survey made at the expense of the three colonies concerned.

This survey, the starting point for the controversies and the proposals of a generation, was completed in 1848, under Major Robinson and Lieutenant Henderson of the Royal Engineers. 'Major Robinson's Line,' as it came to be known, ran roughly in the direction eventually followed by the Intercolonial—from Halifax to Truro, and thence north to Miramichi and the Chaleur Bay, and up the Metapedia Valley to the St Lawrence.

After the plan of a northern route to Quebec was abandoned, interest shifted to the Portland connections. The building of the road from Montreal to Portland added further strength to the claims of this route. The name of the proposed road, the European & North American, expressed the hope that the road from Portland to Halifax would become the channel of communication between the United States and Europe, at least for passengers, mail and express traffic.

In July 1850 a great convention assembled in Portland, attended by delegates from New Brunswick and Nova Scotia as well as from Maine and other New England states. The delegates from the Maritime Provinces returned home full of enthusiasm, but increasingly uncertain about the securing of the necessary capital. At this stage Joseph Howe came to the front. He proposed to seek from the Imperial government a guarantee of the necessary loan, in order that the province might borrow on lower terms. The Colonial Office, while expressing its approval of the Portland scheme, declined to give a guarantee more than a cash contribution. Not daunted, Howe sailed for England in November 1850 and in spite of Cabinet changes in London secured the pledge he desired.

Howe returned triumphant. The British government would guarantee a loan of $35 million which would build the roads to Portland and to Quebec and perhaps still farther west. This railway's importance lay in the fact that it provided a short route between the Province's largest port on the Atlantic and towns on the Bay of Fundy.

Then suddenly the bubble burst. The Colonial Office, late in 1851, declared that Howe had been mistaken in declaring that the guarantee was to extend to the European & North American project. The British government had no objection to this road being built, but would not aid it. The officials of the Colonial Office declared that they never meant to promise anything else. The whole plan thus fell to the ground. The consent of the three provinces was essential, and the New Brunswick would not support the Halifax & Quebec project if the Portland road,

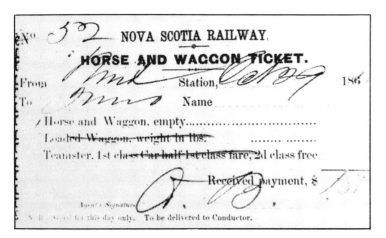

Piggy-back in Nova Scotia, 1855

Piggybacking is nothing new—the ticket *at top, above,* and the illustration *above* clearly show that carrying wagons and their attendant horses was normal for 19th century Canadian railways. Today's piggybacks haul truck trailers and other intermodal containers.

running through the most populous and influential sections of the province, was to be postponed indefinitely. Finance Minister Hincks was determined to save the situation. Accompanied by John Young and EP Taché, he visited Fredericton and Halifax early in 1852, and hammered out a compromise. New Brunswick agreed to join in the Halifax to Quebec project on condition that the road should run from Halifax to St John and thence up the valley of the St John River; Nova Scotia agreed to this change, which made St John rather than Halifax the main ocean terminus, on condition that New Brunswick should bear five-twelfths as against its own three-twelfths of the cost. It remained to secure the consent of the Imperial government and Hincks, Chandler and Howe arranged to sail for England early in March. Upon a peremptory request from Hincks for a definite answer within a fortnight, the British Cabinet, in spite of the previous promise to consider the route an open question, declined to aid any but a road following Major Robinson's line. The negotiations broke off, joint action between the provinces failed, and each province switched to its own separate track.

It was on 13 June 1854 that the first sod was turned for the construction of the Nova Scotia Railway—a beginning made at last. The road was to run from Halifax to Truro, with a branch to Windsor. Progress was slow, but

by 1858 the 93 miles planned had been completed.

The line's track was somewhat unusual in that the iron rails were shaped the same top and bottom; when the top became worn, they were turned upside down.

They also carried an unusual kind of traffic. Before the railway, farmers living near Windsor and Truro had taken produce to Halifax by horse and wagon. To attract them, the Nova Scotia Railway offered to load horse, wagon and driver onto a flat car. In the capital's station, they were unloaded and the wagon went off to market. (Today, railways carry highway trailers on flat cars in a similar type of service called 'piggyback'.)

A halt in progress came when reality succeeded the glowing visions of the prospectus, the service proved poor, and the returns low. Nine years later an extension from Truro to Pictou was constructed.

New Brunswick had a more variable experience. After the collapse of the Halifax & Quebec project, her efforts were confined to the road running north from St Andrews and to the European & North American.

Rail Travel in the Mid-1800s

The first 'age of iron—and of brass' came to an end before 1860. Between 1850 and 1860, the mileage of all the provinces grew from 66 to 2065. By 1867 it had increased only 213 miles. In two of the intervening years not a mile was built. A halt had come, for stock taking and heart searching.

A person—or package—could travel by train all the way from Riviére du Loup in Quebec to Sarnia in Ontario. People who did so found the journey long and tiring. Most rails were only 18 feet long and there was quite a gap between the end of one and the beginning of the next (to prevent the 'snake rails' mentioned previously). As wheels crossed the gaps, cars jolted and passengers bounced. Cushioned seats made first-class travel a little more comfortable, but everyone in second class sat on plain wooden benches. Trains stopped at mealtimes because there were no dining cars. They also stopped for the night, because there were no sleeping accommodations on board, and passengers had to find rooms in hotels.

The first sleeping car in the world was designed and built in Hamilton, Ontario, by the Great Western Railway. It looked like a box car fitted with long benches, and each passenger was given a rug and a pillow. They certainly weren't comfortable, but at least trains could keep rolling through the night, so the journey took less time.

Locomotives used wood for fuel then and, because it burned quickly, trains had to stop every 50 miles to pick up another load, supplies by farmers. When a train was running late, passengers were asked to help bring the wood aboard.

If the trip was difficult for passengers, it was extremely so for train and locomotive crews. The fireman had to keep throwing heavy logs into the fire box and, whenever he had a chance, climb outside onto the engine to grease bearings. It was also his job to load the wood at each stop, and clean ashes out of the fire box.

There were compensations, though. The crews were very popular in the towns they passed through, because they brought news and gossip from other points along a line. Engineers especially were admired. They were idols for children who were learning in school how big the world around them really was, and dreaming of seeing it.

The Building Blocks

The Grand Trunk

The most important railway company established between 1850 and 1860 was the Grand Trunk Railway Company of Canada. Its name stemmed from its purpose: to operate a long, important main line which other, smaller lines would join.

By 1851 the St Lawrence, the Great Western and the Northern were under way, and more ambitious schemes proposed. The Guarantee Act of 1849 was proving inadequate, and the government was considering an extension.

In 1849 Hincks had argued against government ownership; now he argued for it. The new act, passed in April 1852, marked the second or Grand Trunk phase of his gradually shaping policy. The next move was to arrange terms with the other provinces and secure the promised Imperial guarantee.

It is clear, however, that the British government was unwilling to consider anything but the unacceptable Major Robinson line. Hincks was justified in looking elsewhere for capital, but he was not justified in binding himself to one firm of contractors, however eminent, which is what he had done.

Hincks returned to Canada in the summer of 1852 with a tentative contract in his pocket. To Canada, too, came Henry Jackson, a partner in the Brassey Company, the railway-building firm with whom Hincks had associated himself. The supposition of the government was that the English contractors would simply subscribe for the bulk of the stock in these companies, but the Canadian promoters were not willing to give up their rights so easily, and they subscribed for the full $3 million which was authorized. Hincks met this move by bringing down a bill

At right and above right: These Grand Trunk 4–4–0 coalburners were typical of North American motive power in the 1880s. Such engines were often used for both passenger and freight hauling, though their large driving wheels were conducive to building up speed, while engines with comparatively smaller wheels developed better traction.

RAILWAY

At left: This 1870s-era smoke belcher is surrounded by its very proud-looking crew. These fellows were privileged to operate the most advanced means of propulsion available on the planet in their time. The Grand Trunk had tough going in its infancy, but struggled on to do its mother country—Canada—good service. *Above* is an early company logo.

to incorporate a new company, the Grand Trunk Railway Company of Canada, and the rights of the rival claimants came before parliament for decision.

Hincks became alarmed at Montreal interest arrayed against him, and proposed as a compromise that the Grand Trunk should absorb the St Lawrence road and build the bridge at Montreal on the condition that the opposition to its westward plans should be abandoned. Upon this all parties agreed, and the English and Canadian promoters joined forces.

Negotiations were completed in England early in 1853. As yet the Grand Trunk Company was but a name. The real parties to the bargain were many. First came John Ross, a member of the Canadian cabinet, but representing the future Grand Trunk, of which he was elected president. The Barings and Glyns, eminent banking houses, had a twofold part to play, as they were closely connected to the contractors and were also the London agents of the Canadian government. The contractors themselves, Peto, Brassey, Betts and Jackson, had spent a year studying the Canadian situation and put in anxious weeks hammering out the details of the agreement and the prospectus to follow it.

A glowing prospectus was drawn up. The amalgamated road would be the most comprehensive railway system in the world, comprising 1112 miles, stretching from Portland and eventually from Halifax (by both the northern and the southern route) to Lake Huron. The whole future traffic between west and east must therefore pass over the Grand Trunk, as both geographical conditions and legislative enactment prevented it from injurious competition. It was backed by government guarantee and Canadian investment, and its execution was in the hands of the most eminent contractors. The total capital was fixed at $47.5 million.

A M Ross was appointed chief engineer, and S P Bidder general manager, both on the nomination of the English bankers and contractors. Plant was assembled in Canada, orders for rails and equipment were placed in England, and workers came out by the thousand. At one time 14,000 men were directly employed on the railways in upper Canada alone. In July 1853 the last gaps in the

These pages: A freight train stops for water at Coopersville in 1890. Such stops cost time, and were one of the factors that would eventually do in steam locos, as diesels—whose development would follow the scene shown here by some 40–50 years—needed no such stops.

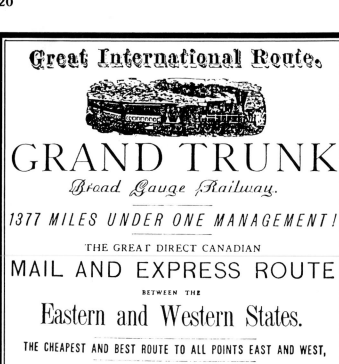

Thomas Edison's printing press could have produced the ad *above* and the ticket *below* (see caption, facing page) but the young inventor was busy publishing the first newspaper on wheels (see text at right).

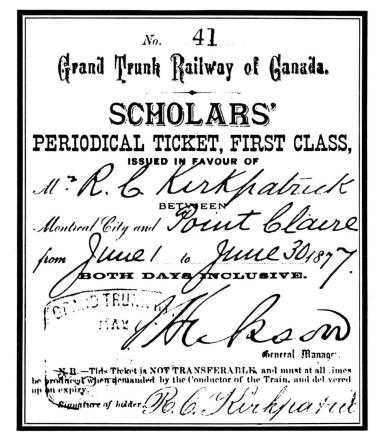

St Lawrence & Atlantic had been filled up, though not permanently. In 1854 the Quebec and Richmond section was opened; in 1855, the road from Montreal to Brockville and from Lévis to St Thomas, Quebec; in 1856, the Brockville to Toronto and Toronto to Stratford sections.

Thousands of people from Toronto, Quebec, Boston and Portland poured into Montreal for the giant party celebrating the completion of the line from Montreal to Toronto in 1856. The city held a parade one morning and gave a banquet for more than 4000 guests. They sat at over 1000 yards of tablecloths and used 88,000 knives, forks, and spoons. The following evening there was a ball but, according to newspaper reports, the hall was so crowded that no one had room to dance until one o'clock in the morning, after some of the people had gone home.

Not until 1858 was the western road completed as far as London. The year 1859 saw the completion of the Victoria Bridge across the St Lawrence at Montreal. Over a mile long, it had only one track when it was opened in 1859, but a second was added during major reconstruction 40 years later. The extension from St Mary's to Sarnia, and a new road on Michigan, running from Port Huron to Detroit were also completed in 1859. Coincidentally, also in 1859, Thomas Alva Edison, inventor of the incandescent light bulb and originator of a host of technological innovations in the fields of telegraphy, sound recording and electricity, began his career on the Chicago, Detroit & and Canada Grand Trunk Junction Railroad as a newsboy and 'candy butcher' or candy seller.

Hired at the age of twelve, Edison worked from morning to midnight on the Port Huron to Detroit run, using spare time during layovers to experiment in baggage car chemistry laboratory. He removed the lab in 1862 after a phosphorous fire set the car ablaze but substituted a printing press for his chemicals. He wrote and printed the first paper ever published on a moving train—The Weekly Herald—and charged three cents a copy.

Success was mixed with tragedy and heroism. An accident while boarding a moving freight on the Port Huron left the young inventor partly deaf. In 1862, Edison's quick action saved the life of Jimmie Mackenzie, the 3-year-old son of the Grand Trunk stationmaster in Mt. Clemens, Michigan. Edison snatched the boy from the path of an oncoming train, and the grateful father, J U Mackenzie, an experienced telegrapher, rewarded him by teaching him to be a telegrapher. This was a turning point in the life of a young Edison. The telegraph key on which he learned his craft is now in Greenfield Village, Dearborn, Michigan. (J U Mackenzie later joined Edison at his New Jersey Menlo Park laboratory and aided in a number of inventions.)

Edison was a telegrapher at the railroad's Stratford Junction, Ontario Station, staying there until 1864, when he resigned. His telegraphy experience created an interest in elementary circuitry that led to his first inventions. Grand Trunk was an impetus toward a great career.

In his biography, Thomas Edison tells of handling the controls of a steam locomotive when he was 15 years old. His unauthorized stint as an engineer was made on *The Arab* in 1862. On several occasions, the regular crew let Edison handle the controls between Port Huron and Mount Clemens, Mich. so they could sleep. The so-called 'Edison line of the Grand Trunk' was the Chicago, Detroit

& Canada Grand Trunk Junction between Port Huron and Detroit built by Grand trunk in 1858–59.

The Grand Trunk was complete from Lake Huron to the Atlantic in 1860. In the 10 years that followed, working expenses varied from 58 to 85 percent of the gross receipts, instead of the 40 percent which the prospectus had foreshadowed; not a cent of dividend was paid on ordinary shares.

The prophecy that operating expenses would not exceed 40 percent of earnings, based on English experience, failed partly because earnings were lower, but more because operating expenses were higher than anticipated. The company had more than its share of hard luck from commercial depression, and from loss on American paper money in the Civil war. Differences in gauge, lack of permanent connections at Chicago, lack of return freight, rate wars with the American railroads which had been built west at the same time or later, the inferiority of Montreal to New York as of old in harbor facilities and ocean service, the failure of Portland to become a great commercial center—all meant hope and dividends deferred.

The Grand Trunk did Canada good service, however. In 1850 there were only 66 miles of road in all of the provinces. In 1860 there were 2065. The Great Western and Northern were pushed forward under the provisions

of the earlier Guarantee Act; roads of more local interest were fostered by municipal rivalry. Their building brought new activity in every branch of commerce.

The Great Western

In Ontario, The Great Western railway started building two lines, one from Hamilton to Niagara Falls and the other from Hamilton to London. The company had actually been formed in 1834, but it was not until the government promised to help that the Great Western could afford to begin laying track.

By 1858, the company was operating 360 miles of rail lines, from Toronto to Windsor, Niagara Falls, and Sarnia. These lines were very important to Canada because they opened up the rich farmlands of southwestern Ontario. As well, they provided rail links with the United States.

The Great Western was a very progressive company. For example, it was the first railway in the world to sort mail *en route*. Later on, special 'Railway Post Office' cars were built, and remained in use until 1971. (Since then, most Canadian inter-city mail has been moved by air.) The Great Western also built the first railway suspension

These pages: The Great Western's early motive power is evident in this vintage photo of the *William Weir*, half out of a station shed. The GW was financially far more successful than the majority of early railroads; perhaps that's why these gents look so pleased with themselves.

bridge, opened to traffic in 1855. Spanning the Niagara River just below the Falls, it was 820 feet long and considered an engineering marvel of the times.

The Great Western came nearest of any early road to being a financial success; alone of the guaranteed roads it repaid the government loan, nearly in full.

The Intercolonial

In 1857, Queen Victoria named Ottawa as the Capital Province of Canada, and during the next decade serious talk about political union of all the British North American colonies began.

Leaders of the four Maritime colonies met in Charlottetown in 1864 to discuss uniting them. A few months later, another conference was held in Quebec to discuss a larger federation, of the Maritimes with the Province of Canada. Railways were not only an important topic at both meetings, but New Brunswick and Nova Scotia refused to participate in the larger plan unless they were promised a rail link with what would become Quebec and Ontario.

Railways were also important to the provinces that joined the Confederation after it became a fact on July 1, 1867, with John A MacDonald as prime minister.

Two years later, Canada bought Prince Rupert's Land from the Hudson's Bay Company and marked out what are today's three Prairie Provinces and the Yukon Territory and Northwest Territories. Manitoba entered Confederation in 1870. Beyond the Rocky Mountains, British Columbia joined in 1871 because it was promised a rail link with the rest of the country—otherwise, it would probably have joined the United States. And Prince Edward Island decided to become a part of Canada in 1873 when it ran out of money to finish building its own railway.

The outstanding achievement of the period after confederation, however, was the building of the Intercolonial. It had been projected largely in order to make closer union between the provinces possible, but, as it turned out, it was Confederation that brought the Intercolonial, not the Intercolonial that brought Confederation.

After the breakdown of negotiations in London in 1852, each province had turned to its own tasks. Each in building its own roads provided possible links in the future Intercolonial chain. In Canada the Grand Trunk ran to a point 120 miles east of Quebec; in New Brunswick, St John was connected with both the east and west boundaries of the province; in Nova Scotia, a road ran north from Halifax as far as Truro. A gap of nearly 500 miles between Rivière du Loup and Truro remained. To bridge this wilderness seemed beyond the private or public resources of the divided provinces. Unanimous on one point only, they once more turned to the British government. In 1857 and 1858 dispatches and deputations sought aid, but sought it in vain. When the Civil War broke out in the United States, official British sympathy was given to the South. In 1861 the British sent 8000 troops to Canada in response to an incident in which Captain Wilks of the Union forces had seized two confederate officers from aboard a ship named *The Trent*.

At right: The Great Western's Great International Railway Suspension Bridge. connecting the United States and Canada—and the New York Central and the Great Western Railways. Opened in 1855, this bridge was the first railroad suspension bridge. Niagra Falls is in the distance.

Above: The Fathers of Confederation —who represented the Maritime colonies in effecting a confederation with provincial Canada on 1 July 1867—held railroad building high on their list of priorities. *At right:* The first locomotive built at Moncton, New Brunswick. Railways provided a vital binding for the nation that would become modern Canada.

The Trent Affair, as it came to be called, showed how near Britain and the North were to war, a war which would at once have exposed isolated Canada to attack. The military argument for closer connection then took on new weight with the British government, and it proposed, to a joint delegation in 1861, to revert to its offer of 10 years earlier—to guarantee a colonial loan for a railway by an approved route. During the progress of the survey negotiations for the union of the provinces had begun, and when Confederation came about in 1867, the building of the Intercolonial at the common expense of the Dominion, with an imperial guarantee to the extent of $15 million, was one of the conditions of the union.

The construction was entrusted in December 1868 to a commission of four, and six years later the minister of public works took over direct control. At last, on July 1876, nine years after Confederation, the 500 miles between Truro and Rivière du Loup were opened for traffic throughout. As branch lines were completed small companies sold their trackage and equipment to larger ones, and thus the Intercolonial acquired the line between Rivière du Loup and Lévis, across the St Lawrence from Quebec City.

In the meantime the Dominion had taken over the Nova Scotia, New Brunswick, and Prince Edward Island government roads. In 1876 there were in all 950 miles of railway under the control of the Dominion government, as against 4268 miles of private lines.

The Canadian Pacific

Unlike most Canadian railroads, the Canadian Pacific was never absorbed by the Canadian National Railway. It remains in business to this day and is now the second-largest railroad in Canada. Its story, however, is important to the history of all Canada's rails—indeed, it is important to the history of all Canada. The construction of the Canadian Pacific opened up the western provinces to many of the smaller lines and industries that eventually became part of CN.

After the coming of the locomotive, one needed only imagination and a map to see all British North America clamped by an iron band. Engineers like Bonnycastle and Synge and Carmichael-Smyth wrote of the possibility in the the 1840s. Promoters were not lacking. But two things were needed before the dreams on paper could become facts in steel—national unity and international rivalry. Years before Confederation, such far-seeing Canadians as William M'Dougall and George Brown had pressed for the annexation of the British territories beyond the Lakes. After Confederation, all speed was made to buy out the sovereign rights of the Hudson's Bay Company. Then came the first Riel Rebellion, to bring home the need of a western road, as the Trent Affair had brought home the need of the Intercolonial. The decisive political factor came into play in 1870, when British Columbia entered the federation.

The other factor, international rivalry, exercised its influence about the same time. In the United States the railway had rapidly pushed westward, but had halted before the deserts and mountains lying between Mississippi and the Pacific. The rivalry of pro-slavery and anti-slavery parties in Congress had deadlocked all plans of public aid to either southern or northern route. Then the Civil War broke the deadlock: the need of binding the West to the side of the North created a strong public demand for a Pacific road, and Congress, so stimulated, gave loans and land grants. The Central Pacific, working from Sacramento, and the Union Pacific, starting from Omaha, met near Ogden in Utah in 1869. In 1871 the Southern Pacific and the Texas Pacific were fighting for subsidies, and Jay Cooke was promoting the Northern Pacific. The young Dominion of Canada was Stirred by ambition to emulate its powerful neighbor.

These factors, then, brought the question of a railway to the Pacific on Canadian soil within the range of practical politics. Important questions remained to be settled. During the parliamentary session of 1871 the government of Sir John MacDonald decided that the road should be built by a company, not by the state, that it should be aided by liberal subsidies in cash and in land, and, to meet British Columbia's insistent terms, that it should be begun within two, and completed within ten, years. The opposition protested that this latter provision was uncalled for and would bankrupt the Dominion, but the government carried its point.

The first task was to survey the vast wilderness between the Ottawa Valley and the Pacific, and to find if possible a feasible route. Explorer and engineer Captain Palliser had been appointed by the British government to report upon the country west of the Lakes. He had declared in 1863, after four years of careful labor in the field, that, thanks to the choice of the 49th parallel as Canada's boundary, there was no possibility of ever building a transconinental railway exclusively through British territory. The man chosen for the task of achieving this impossibility was Stanford Fleming. Appointed engineer-in-chief in 1871, he was for nine years in charge of the surveys, though for half that time his duties on the Intercolonial absorbed much of his energy. Fleming possessed an unusual gift of literary style, and his reports upon the work of his staff gave the people of Canada a very clear idea of the difficulties to be encountered.

Below: The Canadian Pacific's first locomotive, the 4-4-0 woodburner *Countess of Dufferin,* is shown here on display in the 1950s. The locale of this photo is Winnipeg, Manitoba, but the CP's influence had come to be known from coast to coast. *At right:* The *Countess of Dufferin,* with cars, arrives at Winnipeg on 9 October 1877, via a barge pushed by the sternwheeler *Selkirk.* This loco greatly aided the building of the CP.

Early in the survey a practical route was found throughout. Striking across the wilderness from Lake Nipissing to Lake Superior at the Pic River, the line might skirt the shore of the lake to Fort William, or it might run northerly through what is now known as the clay belt, with Fort William and the lake made accessible by a branch. Continuing westward to the Red River at Selkirk, with Winnipeg on a branch line to the south, the projected line crossed Lake Manitoba at the Narrows, and then struck out northwesterly, through what was then termed the 'Fertile Belt', until the Yellowhead Pass was reached. Here the Rockies could be easily pierced; but once through Fleming was faced by the huge flanking range of the Caribou Mountains, in which repeated explorations failed to find a gap. At the foot of the towering barrier lay a remarkable deep-set valley 400 miles in length, in which northwestward ran the Fraser and southeastward the Canoe and Columbia. By following the Fraser to its great southward bend, and then striking west, a terminus on Bute or Dean Inlet might be reached, while the valley of the Canoe and the Albreda would give access to the North Thompson and lower Fraser to Burrard inlet. The latter route, on the whole, was preferred.

It was estimated that the Canadian road would cost $100 million and it was certain that the engineering difficulties would be staggering. In Canada few roads had paid the shareholders, and though some had profited the contractors, the new enterprise meant such a plunge in the dark that contractors and promoters alike hesitated. In the United States, however, the Pacific roads had proved gold mines for their promoters.

In June 1880, Sir John MacDonald, speaking at Bath, made the announcement that a group of capitalists had offered to build the road, on terms that would ensure that in the end it would not cost Canada a single penny. Four months later a contract was signed in Ottawa by which the Canadian Pacific Syndicate undertook to build and operate the whole road. An entirely new turn had been given to the situation, and the most important chapter in Canada's railway annals, if not in her national life had begun.

In the months and years that followed, no men were so much in the mind and speech of the Canadian public as the members of the new syndicate. The leading members were a remarkable group of men. Probably never in the history of a railway building, not even in the case of the 'Big Four' who built the Central Pacific—Huntington, Stanford, Crocker, and Hopkins—had the call of the railway brought together in a single enterprise men of such outstanding individuality, of such ability and persistence, and destined for success so notable.

They were Norman W Kittson, head of a small transportation company; James J Hill, Donald A Smith and George Stephen, pioneers in the true sense who had come West while young to try their luck, and were at the time employed in various respectable but unnotable occupations; and Richard B Angus, a shrewd financier.

The Canadian Pacific was not their first joint enterprise. It was the direct outcome of a daring venture in connection with a bankrupt Minnesota railway, which had brought them wealth beyond their wildest dreams, and had definitely turned their thoughts to railway work.

These were the men to whom the Canadian government turned when the minister of Railways, Sir Charles

Opposite: The first president of the CP. George Stephen, served from 1881–1888. The building of the CP was financially risky, at the least. *Above:* Hudson's Bay chief commissioner Donald A Smith envisioned the railroad's role in building a strong Canadian commerce.

Tupper, urged them to unload upon a private company the burden of completing the road to the Pacific. 'Catch them before they invest their profits,' was the advice of Sir John's most intimate adviser, the shrewd Eastern Townships politician John Henry Pope. Probably they came halfway. They knew the West as well as many men, and with their road built to the Canadian boundary and with a traffic arrangement beyond to Winnipeg, they were already in the field. Of all the group Stephen was most reluctant to undertake the new enterprise, but he was assured by his associates that the burdens of management would be shared by all. The government had also approached Duncan M'Intyre, a Montreal financier who controlled the Canada Central, running from Brockville by way of Ottawa to Pembroke, and under construction from that point to Callender, the eastern end of the Canadian Pacific main line. He was more than willing to link up this railway with the larger project, and the group was formed.

They debated the question with the government early in 1880. It was felt, however, that negotiations could not be concluded in Canada. More capital would be needed than even these new millionaires could furnish, and nowhere was capital so abundant as in London. In July, therefore, Sir John MacDonald, Sir Charles Tupper, and John

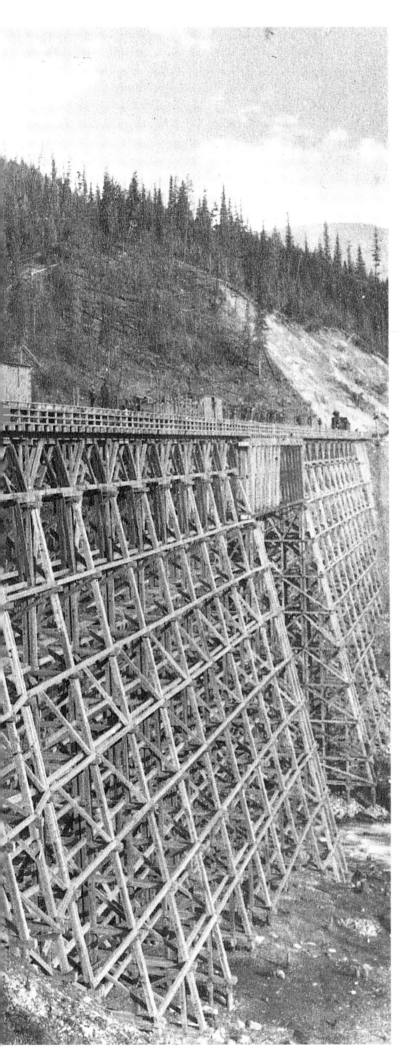

Henry Pope sailed for London, accompanied by George Stephen and Duncan M'Intyre. London financiers did not bite as freely as anticipated. Barings and Rothschilds alike were cautious about the enterprise. Sir Henry Tyler, president of the Grand Trunk, was approached and agreed to build if the link north of Lake Superior were omitted in favor of a line through the United States, south of the lake, a condition which Sir John, strongly urged on by Tupper, would not accept.

The group returned to Ottawa on 21 October 1880, the contract was signed by Charles Tupper for the government and by George Stephen, Duncan M'Intyre, James J Hill, John S Kennedy, Morton, Rose & Company of London, and Cohen, Reinach & Company of Paris. Donald A Smith's name was not there. It was only two years since he and Sir John, on the floor of the House of Commons, had called each other 'liar' and 'coward' and it was to be a few years more before the two Highlanders could cover their private feud with a coating of elaborate cordiality. So, to preserve appearances, Smith's interest was kept a secret—but a very open one.

When Parliament met in December 1880 the contact was laid before it. For constructing some 1900 miles the syndicate would be given free the 710 miles already under construction by the government, $25 million in cash, and 25 million acres of selected land in the Fertile Belt. They were promised exemptions from import duties on construction materials, from taxes on land for 20 years after the patents were issued and on stock and other property forever, and exemption from regulation of rates until 10 per cent per annum was earned on the capital. Assurance was given that for 20 years no competitive roads connecting with the western states would be chartered. Ten years were given to complete the task, and a million dollars were deposited as a security. The contract was ratified by Parliament and received the formal royal assent in February 1881.

George Stephen was chosen president, and held the post until 1888. To him more than to any other man the ultimate success of the Canadian Pacific was due. Indomitable persistence, unquenchable faith and unyielding honor stamped his character. He was one of the greatest of empire builders. He never despaired in the tightest corner and never rested while a single expedient remained untried. Duncan M'Intyre became one of the two vice presidents and took an active part in the company's affairs until he dropped out in 1884. Richard B Angus came back from St Paul to become vice president and a member of the executive committee. His long banking experience and his shrewd, straightforward judgement proved a tower of strength in days of trial.

Donald A Smith, while after 1883 a director and a member of the executive committee, took little part in the railway's affairs, though at Stephen's urging he more than once joined in lending security when help was most needed. James J Hill left the directorate and unloaded his stock at the close of 1882. With him retired John S Kennedy. The Baron de Reinach also withdrew at an early stage. The English directors, representing Morton, Rose & Company of London, retired as soon as the road was

At left: The Canadian Pacific's original engineering marvel, Mountain Creek Bridge, on the eastern slope of the Selkirks. This structure was 164 feet high, 1086 feet long, and contained more than two million board feet of lumber in its intricate underpinnings.

completed, being replaced by representatives of Morton, Bliss & company of New York. E B Osler came in with the Ontario & Quebec in 1884. The board became more and more distinctively Canadian.

One of the first steps taken by the directors was to open offices in Winnipeg, and put two men with United States experience in charge—A B Stickley, later president of Chicago Great Western, as general superintendent, and General Rosser as chief engineer. The rate of progress was not satisfactory, and early in 1882 a fortunate change was made. William C Van Horne, at that time general superintendent of the Chicago, Milwaukee & St Paul and still under age forty, was appointed general manager with wide powers. Some years earlier, when he was president of the Southern Minnesota, the leading members of the St Paul syndicate had had an opportunity of learning his skill. He had been railroading since he was fourteen, beginning as a telegraph operator on the Illinois Central, and had risen rapidly in the service of one Midwest road after another. His tireless driving force was precisely the asset the company now most needed.

Stephen and Smith and M'Intyre pledged their St Paul or other stock for loans in New York and Montreal, but still the financial gap was unfilled. They turned to the government, requesting a loan of $22.5 million, to be secured by a first charge on the main line. In return, they agreed to complete the road by May 1886, five years earlier than the contract required. The request was at first scouted by Sir John MacDonald. Parliament would not consent, and if Parliament consented the country would

Above: This 'track laying machine' was a delivery winch, which hauled rails forward through troughs one side of the construction train, and ties forward through troughs on the other side, saving the 'navvies' legwork. *Below right:* A vintage shot of a new road-cut near Lake Superior.

revolt. Bankruptcy stared the company in the face when John Henry Pope came to the rescue. He soon convinced Sir John that if the Canadian Pacific was smashed, the Conservative party would smash the day after, and the aid was promised. The cabinet was won over, and Sir Charles Tupper, hastily summoned by cable from London, stormed it through caucus, and the loan was made.

The men behind the Canadian Pacific proved themselves possessed of courage and honorable determination. At more than one critical stage they staked their all to keep the work going even though the bulk of the resources used in the original building of the road were provided or advanced by the people of Canada. The Canadian Pacific is a monument of public as well as of private faith.

Meanwhile the work of construction had been going ahead. Under William Van Horne's masterful methods the leisurely pace of government construction quickened to the most rapid achievement on record. A time schedule, carefully made out in advance, was adhered to with remarkably little variation.

Work was begun at the east end of the line, from the point of junction with the Canada Central, but at first energy was devoted chiefly to the portion crossing the plains. Important changes in route were made. The main line had already been deflected to pass through Winnipeg. Now a much more southerly line across the plains was adopted, making for Calgary rather than Edmonton. The new route was shorter by 100 miles, and more likely to prevent the construction of a rival road south of it later. For many years it had been assumed that the tillable lands of the West lay in a 'Fertile Belt' or rainbow, following roughly the Saskatchewan Valley and curving round a big wedge of the American desert projecting north. Certainly the short, withered, russet-colored grasslands of the border country looked forbidding beside the green herbage of North Saskatchewan. But new investigations reported in 1879 showed that only a very small section was hopelessly arid. With this objection removed, the only drawback to the southern route was the difficulty of finding as good a route through the mountains as the northerly Yellowhead Pass route, but on this the company decided to take its chances.

Engineering difficulties on the plains were not serious, but the pace of construction which was demanded, and the fact that every stick of timber and every pound of food, as well as every rail and spike, had to be brought a great distance, required remarkable organization. Three hundred subcontractors were employed on the portion of the line crossing the plains. Bridge gangs and track layers followed close on the graders' heels. In 1882 over two-and-a-half miles of track a day were laid. In the following year, for weeks in succession, the average ran three-and-a-half miles a day, and in a record smashing three days 20 miles were covered. By the end of the year the track was within four miles of the summit of the Rockies.

The change of route across the plains had made it essential to pierce the Rockies by a more southerly pass than the Yellowhead. The Kicking Horse or Hector Pass, short but steep, was finally chosen.

It was not until 1884 that the wilderness north of Lake Superior was attacked in strong force. Nine thousand men were employed here alone. Rock and muskeg, hill and hollow, made this section more difficult to face than even the Fraser Canyon. In one muskeg area seven layers of Canadian Pacific rails are buried, one below the other. The stretch along the shore of the lake was particularly difficult. The Laurentian rocks were the oldest known to geologists and, more pertinent, the toughest known to engineers. A dynamite factory was built on the spot and a road blasted through. One mile cost $700,000 to build and several cost half a million. The time required and the total expenditure would have been prohibitive had not the management decided to make extensive use of trestle work. It would have cost over two dollars a cubic yard to cut through the hills and fill up the hollows by team haul; it cost only one tenth of that to build timber trestles, carrying the line high, and to fill up later by train haul.

In 1885, thousands of Chinese laborers working on the difficult Kamloops-Port Moody section finished their task, and the government work was done. The only gap remaining lay in the Gold Range. There, in the Eagle Pass at Craigellachie, on 7 November 1885, the eastward and westward track layers met. It was only a year or so before that the Northern Pacific had celebrated the driving of the last golden spike by an excursion which cost the company a third of a million dollars and heralded the bankruptcy of the road. There was no banquet and no golden spike for the last rail in the Canadian Pacific. William Van Horne had announced that 'the last spike would be just as good an iron spike as any on the road,'and had it not been that Donald A Smith happened along in time to drive the spike home, it would have been hammered in by the

worker on the job. Six months later the first passenger train went through from Montreal to Vancouver. The longest railway in the world was opened from coast to coast, five years before the time required by the original contract.

To realize how great a work had been accomplished requires today some effort of the imagination. The Canada the present generation knows is a united Canada, an optimistic, self-confident Canada, with rapidly rounding-out industries which give scope for the most ambitious of her sons as well as for tens of thousands from overseas. It is a Canada whose provinces and whose railroads stretch from ocean to ocean. But the Canada of 1870 was much different. On the map it covered half a continent, but in reality it stopped at the Great Lakes. There was little national spirit, little diversity of commercial enterprise.

The Canadian Pacific Railway changed the face of Western Canada. Towns had sprung up all along its route. Winnipeg and Vancouver became cities; farms were spread across the prairies; mining and lumber companies were formed in British Columbia.

Certainly not least among the makers of Canada were the men who undertook that doubtful enterprise and carried it through every obstacle to success.

The Expansion of the Grand Trunk: The Grand Trunk Pacific

In the East, however, many small lines were finding it hard to stay in business. There were nearly 200 of them, most with only a few miles of track, and the population of the young country could not support them all. The Grand trunk bought up many of the lines and by 1900 owned more than 3000 miles of track, mostly in Quebec and Ontario. Among the lines it took over was the Great Western.

The year 1883 saw the high-water mark of prosperity for Grand Trunk. In that year dividends were paid not only on guaranteed but on first, second, and third preference stock.

In 1895 Sir Henry Tyler resigned from the presidency after 23 years of service. His place was taken by Sir Charles Rivers-Wilson, who had a record of efficient service on the borders of politics and finance. The new president and a committee of directors made a thorough investigation of the Grand Trunk and recommended some immediate improvements. Their chief contribution to its success, however, was the discovery of Charles M Hays.

The great rival of the Grand Trunk had pressed forward to prosperity under the driving power of an American general manager. The new administration decided that it, too, would look to the United States for a chief executive of the ruthless efficiency and modern methods which the crisis demanded. They found him in the man who had pulled the Wabash out of a similar predicament. Hays was not quite forty when in 1895 he was appointed general manager. His presence was soon felt.

Equipment was overhauled, larger freight cars were ordered and new terminals acquired. The main bridges on the road—the suspension at Niagara Falls, the International at Fort Erie, and the Victoria at Montreal—were all

At right: The party surveying the route for the Grand Trunk Pacific sets out from their camp near Mount Robson, British Columbia in the early 1900s. At the western terminus of the rails through this rugged scenery, the seaport city of Prince Rupert, British Columbia, was born.

Above: Track layers join east and west in the early 20th century. The gantry at photo left is an early machine called a grasshopper. which emplaced rails and ties after the laborers had prepared the trackbed.

rebuilt on a larger scale between 1896 and 1901. The double tracking of the main line from Montreal westward was continued, and many of the sharp curves and heavy grades of the original construction were revised.

The rush to the Klondike in 1897 started a rate war between the Canadian Pacific and the Grand Trunk, with its American connections, which lasted nearly a year. In its course rates were cut in the East as well as in the West and the Canadian Pacific sent its westbound freight from Toronto by Smith's Falls rather than the direct line of the Grand Trunk to North Bay. Peace was patched up, but the Canadian Pacific shortly afterwards set about building a road of its own from Toronto north to its main line, thus threatening the Grand Trunk with permanent loss of western business, and providing it with one incentive toward the great westward expansion it was soon to undertake.

In 1902 Hays announced that the directors were considering building a line from North Bay, through New Ontario westward, to a terminus on the Pacific at Port Simpson or Bute Inlet. It would be a line of the highest standards. Government aid, the announcement continued, would certainly be sought and expected. However, 1903

was not 1873, and Hays had learned on the Wabash and on the Grand Trunk how difficult it was for a second-class road to compete and how costly was the process of rebuilding with the line in operation.

The Grand Trunk Pacific was organized as a subsidiary company of the old Grand Trunk, which secured control of ownership of all but a nominal share of the $25 million common stock given it in return for guaranteeing part of the Pacific bonds. Only $20 million preference capital stock was provided for, and this was not issued. The interest of the independent shareholder was thus negligible. The money required was secured by the issue of bonds and debenture loans guaranteed by the government or the Grand Trunk.

On the western section a good route through the prairies was decided upon, not without vigorous protest from the Canadian Pacific because of the close paralleling of its line. After repeated surveys of the Peace, Pine, Wapiti, and Yellowhead Passes, the last was chosen, and a line was settled upon down the Fraser and Skeena valleys, passing through two million acres of fertile land.

From Edmonton to Yellowhead Pass in British Columbia the lines of the Canadian Northern and the Grand Trunk Pacific were very close to each other, following the same route through the Rockies. The Grand Trunk Pacific, however, did not go south to Vancouver but in-

stead continued west. Kaien Island, 550 miles north of Vancouver, was chosen as the terminus, rather than Port Simpson as originally designed, and soon on its magnificent harbor and most unpromising site of rock and muskeg the new and scientifically planned seaport city of Prince Rupert began to rise.

As the main line ran far to the north of the St Lawrence lake and river system, the original plan provided for the construction of branch lines to Fort William, North Bay and Montreal. Of these only the first, aided by the Dominion and also by the Ontario government, was built. Later, in 1914, the Dominion government itself decided to build the Montreal branch.

The great Canadian railway companies are much more than railways. The Grand Trunk system, in its new expansion, branched into every neighboring field which could be made to increase the traffic. It (as well as the Canadian Northern) crossed the Prairies roughly 200 miles north of the Canadian Pacific. People were just beginning to settle in these northern parts of Alberta and Saskatchewan so very few towns had as yet been established. To encourage new farming communities, the Grand Trunk Pacific decided to build a railway station every 15 miles along its line, in the hope that new settlements would grow up around them. That particular distance was chosen so that farmers living along the line would have no more than 7-and-a-half miles to travel to deliver their wagonloads of grain.

Stations were given names in alphabetical order from East to West. In many cases, towns did develop around them, taking their names from the railway station. Today, you find names such as Atwater, Bangor and Cana, or Unity, Very, and Winter, all neatly in order along the railway's route.

Many other western towns were named after railway people—conductors, engineers, superintendents, or company directors. One of the more unusual place names in Saskatchewan is Hemaruka. It comes from the first names of the four daughters of a railway vice-president: 'He' is for Helen, 'ma' for Margaret, 'ru' for Ruth, and 'ka' for Kathleen.

This line was very expensive to build. The Grand Trunk had to borrow huge sums of money from England; now it was deep in debt.

The early 20th century also saw a setback for the Grand Trunk. It has been almost 75 years since the 'invincible' Titanic slipped to a watery grave off the coast of Newfoundland on its maiden voyage from Liverpool, England, to New York. Among the 1503 passengers and crew who perished in the 15 April 1912 disaster was Charles Hays. To one extent or another, Hays' death altered the course of railroad history.

Hays had gone to England to discuss construction of the Southern New England Railroad with British financiers, who had underwritten much of the expense for building the Grand Trunk. It was his dream to extend the Grand Trunk-owned trackage from the Central Vermont at Palmer, Massachusetts, to Providence, Rhode Island, (and ultimately to Boston) to provide a deep-water port in the US for the import of Canadian-bound trade and the export of Canadian products.

Governor Aram Pothier of Rhode Island, a native of Woonsocket, was a strong advocate of the SNE and personally took the controls of a massive steam shovel during groundbreaking ceremonies on 11 May 1912, three weeks after Hays died.

However, without Hays' leadership, the project was plagued by one setback and problem after another—not the least of which was the fact that New York financier J P Morgan and New Haven Railroad owner Charles Mellen opposed any intrusion by Grand Trunk into a territory serviced by railroads in which they had substantial financial interests.

War clouds were hovering over Europe and the outbreak of World War I on 28 July 1914 brought to an end the somewhat-tenuous support of the SNE project by British financiers. By 1915, all construction ended and the SNE started fading into history. It took another 16 years to untangle a maze of legal and monetary problems. On 30 January 1931, the receivership of SNE was officially discharged ... ending forever the elegant vision of railroad pioneer Charles Hays.

At the same time as the Grand Trunk Pacific was being built, the Canadian Government was laying track for another very long line from Moncton, New Brunswick, to Winnipeg. This was the National Transcontinental, to run far north of Montreal and Toronto, through wilderness filled with lakes and swamps. Finding the best route was extremely difficult.

At the time it was built, there were practically no settlers living that far north of the St Lawrence River and the Great Lakes. Still, the National Transcontinental Railway did establish a short route to the West and, when valuable minerals were found in several areas there, it was used to ship many thousands of ton of ore to ports and smelters in Quebec and Ontario.

The discovery of gold in the Klondike in the 1880s afforded good advertising for Canada. In government, finance, industry, and the railway were men who rose to the opportunity: no longer was Canada's light hid under a bushel of wheat. The most was made of the alluring gifts she had to offer. Men the world over who strove to better themselves began the flood of immigration.

The first result of the swarming of thousands to the West was a demand for new railways, to open up plain and prairie and mineral range, and to make connection between East and West. The building of the railways in its turn gave a stimulus to every industry. As in the early 1850s and early 1880s, this period of rapid railway expansion was an era of optimistic planning and feverish speculation.

First to seize the golden opportunities was the group of men who built the Canadian Northern. Railway history offers no more remarkable record than the achievement of

At left: The overstuffed, luxurious interior of a Victorian-era passenger coach.

44

The Canadian Pacific couldn't meet the challenge presented by the rapidly growing western territories of the early 1900s, so William Mackenzie (at top) and Donald Mann (above) seized the opportunity and built the Canadian Northern. At right: Grand Trunk locomotive number 2365, in 1889.

these few men, who, beginning in 1895 with a charter for a railway 100 miles long in Manitoba leading nowhere in particular, succeeded in building in 20 years a road from ocean to ocean, and in keeping it in their own hands through all difficulties.

It was in 1895 that William Mackenzie and Donald Mann, along with two fellow contractors, James Ross and H S Holt, decided to buy some of the charters of projected western roads and to build on their own account. They secured the charter of the Lake Manitoba Railroad & Canal Company, carrying a Dominion subsidy of 6000 acres a mile for a line from Portage la Prairie to Lake Manitoba and Lake Winnipegosis. They induced the Manitoba government to add a valuable guarantee of bonds and exemption from taxes. In 1896 running rights were secured over the track of the Manitoba & Northwestern from Portage to Gladstone, and construction was pushed 100 miles northwest from Gladstone to

Dauphin. The coming need of the West was an outlet from Winnipeg to Lake Superior, to supplement the Canadian Pacific. Accordingly in 1898, under powers given by Dominion, Ontario, and Minnesota charters, construction was begun both at Winnipeg and near Port Arthur. Three years later the line was completed. Meantime the earlier road had branched westerly at Sifton, and by 1900 had crossed the border into Saskatchewan at Erwood. In 1899, in amalgamation with the Winnipeg Great Northern, chartered and subsidized to Hudson Bay, the name of the combined roads was changed to the Canadian Northern.

Then came the coup which first made the public and rival railways realize the ambitious reach of the plans of the new railway. In 1888, when the ban upon competition southward with the Canadian Pacific had been lifted, the Northern Pacific had entered Manitoba. It had gradually built up a system of three hundred and twenty

miles, but had not given the competition looked for, dividing traffic with the Canadian Pacific rather than cutting rates. Now the parent line was in the receiver's hands, and its straits gave the Manitoba government its opportunity. It leased for 999 years all the Manitoba lines of the Northern Pacific, but decided it could not profitably operate them itself without connection with the lakes. The only question was whether to lease them again to the Canadian Pacific or to the Canadian Northern . After a lively contest the younger road secured the prize. At a stroke it thus obtained extensive terminals in Winnipeg, a line south to the American border, branches westward through fertile territory and a link which practically closed the gap between its eastern and western roads.

The Canadian Northern had now become the third largest system in Canada, stretching from Lake Superior to Saskatchewan, with nearly 1300 miles in operation in 1902. The feeders were extending through the rich farming lands of the West. The line to Port Arthur supplemented the Canadian Pacific, providing a second spout to the funnel. This merely local success, however, did not long content its promoters. They announced their intention to build from sea to sea. The Grand Trunk, the Trans-Canada and the Great Northern all planned extensive projects.

In 1902 and 1903 a junction of forces between the Grand Trunk and the Canadian Northern was proposed, and would have had much in its favor. The negotiators could not come to terms, however, and each road continued on its independent plan. Undaunted by the Canadian government's decision to recognize and aid the Grand Trunk, the Canadian Northern turned to a policy of piecemeal construction, seeking aid from the provinces as well as from the Canadian government. The Canadian Northern pressed forward extensions, flung out branches, filled in gaps on every side.

By 1905, the year Saskatchewan and Alberta entered Confederation, Canadian Northern lines had crossed the Prairies to Edmonton. Track was laid quickly and perhaps not too well, because MacKenzie and Mann were in a hurry to get things moving. They did, however, keep upgrading it to meet the demands of use as traffic increased.

The Canadian Northern was known as 'the farmers' railway', because it served the often isolated people of the prairies as individuals even while earning money from them. There is a story about one of its trains stopping near a cabin and staying there so long that a passenger asked the conductor about the delay. He explained that the woman who lived in the cabin down the line had to sell two dozen eggs, but she was an egg short so the train had to wait until a hen laid one.

On one occasion a train struck a heifer, breaking its legs. The crew knew from experience that the farmer would make a claim against the railway for the animal without taking into account the additional value of its meat. So a brakeman who had been a butcher quickly killed and dressed it, the carcass and hide were put in the baggage car, sold that same day, and after the farmer's claim was paid in full there were four dollars left for the company.

In Ontario the gap north of Lake Superior was bridged by a line from Port Arthur to Sudbury, not completed until 1914. Toronto and Ottawa were linked with the western lines, and several feeders were acquired which gave connection with Kingston and Brockville.

Having reached Edmonton, Mackenzie and Mann saw the Pacific as their next goal. That, of course, meant building in the mountains, which was much more difficult than on the flat central plain. Surveys for a road from Yellowhead Pass to Vancouver by Sandford Fleming's old route were begun in 1908. By the aid of lavish guarantees and subsidies this last link in the transcontinental system was pushed to completion in 1915.

The men behind the Canadian Northern not only planned such a project, but carried it through, displaying at every stage of the project a mastery of political diplomacy, and untiring persistence, and great financial resourcefulness.

Dominion and province vied in aid which took many forms. In 1894 Canada had abandoned its policy of giving land grants, but the original companies which combined to form the Canadian Northern had previously been promised and later received over four million acres. Up to 1914 about $18 million had been realized from the sale of parts of this land, and the grants unsold were worth millions more. In addition, Ontario gave two million acres and Quebec one-third as much. The Liberal government of Sir Wilfrid Laurier voted cash to aid in building the link between Winnipeg and Lake Superior. It declined to recognize or aid the extension to the Pacific coast, but in 1912 the Conservative government of Sir Robert Borden gave over $6 million for this work, and in the following year $15 million more for the Ontario and western Alberta sections of the main line. The provinces were less lavish; Quebec, Ontario, and Manitoba offered a total of six million.

In 1896, the Canadian Northern was a railway 100 miles long, beginning and ending nowhere, and operated by thirteen men and a boy. In 1914, a great transconinental system was practically completed, over ten thousand miles in length, and covering seven of Canada's nine provinces. The impossible had been achieved.

Below: The Canadian Northern was known as 'the Farmers' Railroad.'

The Grand Trunk, Great Western, and Northern roads owed the old province of Canada on 1 July 1867 $20 million for principal advanced and over $13 million for interest. Other roads were indebted to Canadian municipalities nearly $10 million for principal alone. There had been waste and mismanagement, but the railways had brought indirect gain that more than offset the direct loss. Farming districts were opened up rapidly, freights were reduced in many sections, intercourse was facilitated, and land values were raised.

In the first 30 years of Canadian railway development no question aroused more interest than that of the gauge to be adopted. The width of the carts used in the English coal mines centuries ago determined the gauge of railway track and railway cars over nearly all the world. When the steam locomotive was invented, and used upon the coal-line tramways, it was made of the same four-foot-eight-and-a-half-inch gauge. In England, in spite of the preferences for a seven-foot gauge, the narrower width soon triumphed, though the Great Western did not entirely abandon its wider track until 1892. In Canada the struggle was longer and more complicated.

It was a question on which engineers differed. Speed, steadiness, cost of track construction and cost of maintenance were all to be considered, and all were diversely estimated. In early years, before the need of standardizing equipment was felt, many experiments were made, especially in the United States. In the southern states five feet was the usual width, and the Erie was built on a gauge of six feet, to fit an engine bought at a bargain. But in the United States, as in England, the four-foot-eight-and-a-half-inch width was dominant, and would have been adopted in Canada without question except that local interest, appealing to patriotic prejudice, succeeded in clouding the issue.

But experience proved that it was impossible to maintain different gauges in countries so closely connected as Canada and the United States. As roads became consolidated into larger systems, the inconvenience of different gauges became more intolerable. The expedients of lifting cars bodily to other trucks, of making axles adjustable, and even of laying a third rail, proved unsatisfactory. Late in the 1860s and early in the 1870s the Great Western and the Grand Trunk had to adopt the four-foot-eight-and-a-half-inch gauge only, and other lines gradually followed.

The Canada Southern was built in 1873, running between Fort Erie, opposite Buffalo, and Amherstburg on the Detroit River. It was controlled by the Vanderbilt interests and operated in close cooperation with their other roads, the Michigan Southern, Michigan Central, and New York Central. The Great Western met this attack upon its preserves by building in the same year the Canada Air Line, from Glencoe near St Thomas, to Fort Erie, giving more direct connection with Buffalo. Both roads made use of the magnificent International Bridge, built across the Niagara in 1873 under Grand Trunk control.

An interesting experiment, motivated by the same desire for cheap pioneer construction which in Ontario brought in the narrow gauge, was the wooden railway built in 1870 from Quebec to Gosford. The rails were simply strips of seasoned maple, fourteen feet by seven inches by four inches, notched into the sleepers and wedged in without the use of a single iron spike. The engines and wheels were made wide to fit the rail. In spite of its cheap construction the road did not pay, and the hope of extending it as far as Lake St John was deferred for a generation. A similar wooden railway was built from Drummondville to L'Avenir.

The St Clair Tunnel

Bridging the 19th and 20th Centuries

Close to a century ago, in an age of grand engineering projects, a railroad tunnel was completed under the St Clair River linking the United States and Canada—the world's first international submarine railroad tunnel. Employing innovative construction methods, the tunnel was completed in a relatively short time, the two bores from opposite shores meeting only a fraction of an inch off center. First employing steam locomotive power, the tunnel was later wired for electric operation until the diesel retired it in the 1950s, thus making the St Clair one of the few railroad tunnels in the world to use three types of motive power—perhaps the only tunnel with this distinction.

The St Clair Tunnel has many firsts to its credit. When completed in 1891 it was the largest submarine tunnel in North America. It was the first underwater tunnel built using the shield method of construction and, in fact, was such an engineering achievement that it was widely acclaimed throughout the world in scientific journals as well as the press, rivaling in international attention the Eiffel Tower of 1889.

The story of the St Clair Tunnel begins in the cold mists of a prehistoric ice age when a great glacier carved out the Great Lakes, creating those immense bodies of fresh water so vital in a far future to establish a vast inland waterborne transportation system but establishing physical barriers for road and rail.

As commerce gravitated to the waterways, strategically located cities such as Chicago, Detroit, Toronto and Milwaukee grew fueled by the movement of grain, lumber and people. The Port Huron-Sarnia area was tied closely to shipping, the natural result of an advantageous position at the southern end of Lake Huron. The transportation industry, an economic mainstay of the two cities almost from the start, included ship building, repair yards, ferries, tug boats, piloting, chandlers and sail lofts. When steel rails began pushing their way west, it was inevitable that

these lake ports would also become railroad terminals. By the 1850s the Great Western Railway of Canada completed a line into Point Edward, Ontario, then a small community at the confluence of Lake Huron, and the St Clair river. On the Michigan shore in 1859 rails were spiked down on a line between Detroit and Fort Gratiot, now a section of Port Huron. This trackage was incorporated as the Chicago, Detroit & Canada Grand Trunk Junction Railroad, and later became a component of the Grand Trunk system.

Even before 1859 there was lively traffic across the river and a fleet of ferries was then in service.

The Grand Trunk devised a solution for moving railroad cars across the swift river when it became apparent that transhipping people and goods from cars to wharves to ferries to wharves to cars was a slow and uneconomical process. It used a swing ferry, that is, a ferry that had no on-board propulsion system but depended on the force of the current to push it back and forth as it swung tethered to an anchor placed a considerable distance upstream. The swing ferry was an environmentalist's dream—no smoke, fumes or noise, and it certainly was easy on fuel and repair bills. But this method must have posed problems in the spring when ice floes choked the river and there surely were problems with other shipping. Nevertheless, the swing ferry remained in service for thirteen years and was retired in 1872.

Her successor, *International II*, was perhaps not quite as unusual, only slightly so. She was a gem of technological innovation, being the first propeller-driver carferry on the Great Lakes and the first carferry to carry three sets of tracks on her decks. *International II* wasn't the complete solution to the physical barrier of the broad St Clair River, however. Limited car-carrying capacity, combined with growing traffic demands and the continuing problem of

At right: A 3000hp Grand Trunk Western road switcher emerges from the St Clair Tunnel—which was, when built, the world's first international submarine railroad tunnel, and stretches from Ontario to Michigan.

ice, were creating a backlog of cars on both sides of the river, some of them carrying perishable meat and produce. Another means for crossing the water barrier was needed, and soon. The climate at the time was excellent for a bold scheme to break the barrier at the St Clair River.

The Grand Trunk considered both a bridge and a tunnel. Although a bridge was a logical solution and was given serious consideration, there were problems with the concept.

Both sides of the river are low and flat so a very high bridge with long and expensive approaches would have been required to allow the tall masts of sailing vessels to pass underneath. A draw or lift bridge was ruled out because constant marine traffic would have placed it out of railroad service most of the time, at least during the navigation season. Probably the strongest reasons for abandoning the idea of a bridge were legal and political opposition from shipping interests who not only feared that a bridge would restrict the passage shipping but also because marine operators opposed any construction by transportation rivals threatening to waterborne commerce. So the tunnel option was settled upon, a courageous decision in the face of the failure of an earlier tunnel attempt at Detroit.

The prime mover of the project, Sir Henry Tyler, president of the Grand Trunk, was a business leader who liked to take calculated risks in order to turn a good profit. As an added stimulus, British investors, the majority shareholders in the Grand Trunk, although making a good profit from their shares, desired even larger returns and complained about the slow and conservative pace of the company. Tyler could, therefore, with one move solve both his internal management problem and the challenging river crossing bugbear. And he did, but not without an unsettling beginning. Learning from the Detroit tunnel failure, benefiting from the newest tunneling technology and from the experience provided by the recently-built New York subway system, Tyler engaged an engineer, Walter Shanley, to study the project. Initially, Shanley's charter was to look at both bridge and tunnel concepts and he made test borings in the most obvious place, the narrows at the head of the river where the swing ferry and its successor operated. He found that the subsoil structure was unsuitable for either project and declared that a bridge could never be built on the site. (Sixty years later the Blue Water Bridge opened to motor traffic in that same location). Nevertheless, the tunnel idea persisted and in 1884 the Grand Trunk incorporated a Canadian subsidiary, The St Clair Frontier Tunnel Co, to construct and operate a tunnel, and in 1886 a similar corporation in Michigan, the Port Huron Railroad Tunnel Co. A fifty-year bond in the sum of $2,500,000 was floated (it was then the largest mortgage ever negotiated in Michigan) and the project was under way.

There was little lost time from this point on. There were no environmental impact statements to file in those free-wheeling days and within a few months of incorporation, a new site was selected and new test holes bored. Fortunately, a talented engineer, Joseph Hobson, was put in charge as project engineer. By one account there was reason for haste to complete the tunnel: the Grand Trunk had a lucrative trade carrying meat from the packing house in Chicago to the East, but the shippers were con-

The St Clair Tunnel was completed on 30 August 1890. With both success and tragedy in the tunnel, the Grand Trunk continued briefly to ferry passengers and vehicles across the Saint Clair River with such ferries as the *Grand Haven* *(above)*. Marine transport would come into use again—to compensate for the tunnel's narrow dimensions—in the 1970s.

cerned with delays at Port Huron and were threatening to find another route if shipments could not be expedited.

Construction sites were surveyed on opposite sides of the river and excavation began, but a setback occurred before the drifts progressed far. The problems of quicksand, methane and water seepage proved to be too much and the project was temporarily abandoned. The Canadian cut extended 186 feet, but on the US side where the problem was more severe, the cut reached a length of only 20 feet. Excavations were made with standard techniques of the time but these were not good enough. New technical solutions were essential.

The difficulty was caused in part by the strategy for the tunnel which made good economic sense, but was tricky to execute. The tunnel would be cut through a layer of blue clay and had to be bored with considerable precision since just below the clay was bedrock and not far above it coursed the cold waters of the river. By drilling through the clay, blasting would be unnecessary and forward progress swift. Unfortunately, the clay bed wasn't quite uniform, with water strata and areas of quicksand leading to so much seepage that the pumps were unable to clear water from the bore.

New financing was arranged and a request for bids was issued but there were no takers because of the failure of

the Detroit tunnel and the ill luck of the first attempt at Port Huron-Sarnia. Now Tyler and the tunnel company would have to do it themselves.

Hobson decided to apply three technical innovations in combination, the first company in North America to use this arrangement. It was this technology that brought the tunnel to the attention of scientists and engineers worldwide.

The most important of these innovations was Hobson's use of the Beach hydraulic tunneling shield. Just as a cookie cutter with a sharp edge might be pressed through soft material, the shield method of tunneling would cut through the blue clay under the St Clair River. Two shields were used, each a massive eighty-ton cylinder twenty-one feet seven inches in diameter and sixteen feet long. Built of one-inch thick steel plates, the shield was pushed forward by 24 hydraulic rams spaced around its circumference. A specially-designed circular crane was attached at the rear of the shield to position the half-ton permanent sections of tunnel casing in place after the shield had been pushed forward and the clay removed by hand.

The other solutions for attacking the relatively soft, water-gassy ground were the use of compressed air during construction and a permanent cast iron casing for the tunnel's walls. Conventional wisdom was upset by the use of iron linings instead of traditional bricks and mortar. A more serious drawback, insufficient knowledge of the effects of working under two or three atmospheres of pressure, was limited. The lining performed superbly, but the little-understood problems of working under pressure

resulted in the death of three laborers, several horses and a few mules. The hydraulic shields attracted much popular attention and there were countless lithographs and engravings of them. Few had been built up to this time and then only of very small dimensions. Because engineer Hobson could not obtain drawings of the original shield developed by the British engineer Greathead, he designed his shields on the basis of a few small drawings found in a book. Hobson's shields were almost twice the size of Greathead's. To limit the possibility of a disaster, the vertical shafts were dug at both river banks to start tunneling before digging the expensive approaches. Before reaching the proper depth, fluid clay and silt floated into the diggings faster than it could be removed.

Now a more thorough beginning was made with long and wide approach cuts several thousand feet back from the portals, after which brick bulkheads with air locks were built and the underground construction pushed forward. No underwater tunnel had ever been driven as swiftly. The average monthly headway for both the Canadian and American bores totalled 455 feet and the tunnel was driven through, though not completed, in just one year.

Other new technologies contributed to this unusual and unexpected speed. Electric arc lights were used from the start and telephone communications were also employed. Within the tube, work progressed continuously. Dirt shoveled by hand into small flat cars pulled by mules was removed for two feet ahead of the shield, then the hydraulic jacks pushed the shield forward and the circular

Above: This 0–10–0 engine is typical of those Baldwin designed for use in the St Clair Tunnel. These 'steamers' were replaced with Baldwin-designed electrics in 1908, as smoke and gas accumulation in the tunnel resulted in several deaths by asphyxiation, despite the (Grand Trunk subsidiary) St Clair Tunnel Company's careful safety planning.

cast iron casing, each ring consisting of thirteen 1,000-pound pieces, was bolted into place behind it. Each segment was eighteen inches wide and two inches thick and had been made rust resistant by heating to 400 degrees followed by immersion in pitch. As the shields cut their way forward under the river, water leakage increased but the Ingersoll air compressors at each entrance forced the water and quicksand back and work continued.

The restricted area inside the tunnel shafts certainly could have provided a chapter for Dante's *Inferno*. Tunnel crews consisted of 75 men per shift—26 diggers, 15 section or casing workers, and the rest at various jobs such as mule skinning. Men and mules, working shoulder to shoulder in the foul air under the glare of arc lamps, were covered with blue mud under conditions of 100 percent humidity. The noise level must have been deafening and odors formidable. Added to this was the ever-present danger of a blowout, which would lead to flooding the tunnel. There also was the little understood danger of working under pressure. On the positive side, however, was the increased pay of an extra dollar a day for working under pressurized air conditions and the fact that temperatures in the tunnel remained in the fifties no matter how hot it was outside. So close were the tolerances through the blue clay that workers could hear propellers of steamships passing overhead.

It was routinely expected that an engineering project of any magnitude would take its toll of human lives—it was part of project costs and indeed costs of fatalities in those days of no liability and minor insurance coverage was neg-

ligible, except, of course, to the families of the victims. Working conditions on the railroads of the time were no better and probably switchmen and trainmen suffered as many casualties—maiming and fatalities—as did the troops involved in any of the small colonial wars of the period. Although railroading was a hazardous occupation, there was an extra dimension of danger in tunnel work with the threats of cave-ins, flooding and explosive misfires. The St Clair tunnel added the basic dangers of being underwater and of being driven through ground saturated with methane. To protect against methane and to hold back the blue clay and the cold waters of the St Clair River, the tunnel was pressurized from ten to thirty-four pounds per square inch above normal atmospheric pressure. Pressure varied depending on the degree of seepage and consistency of the clay.

In the 1880s pressurized tunnel work was still a new technique and little was known about the physical effects of working under pressure. With reasonable care, laborers were not excessively bothered or harmed, at least in the short term. The pressure was too great for horses, however, which initially were used to haul trains of flats removing the excavated material. Mules mostly survived where horses quickly died. There are no reports on whether or not the mules were given a period of slow decompression—it would be interesting to know if they did—but the men were all instructed on the need for this process, which they apparently did on their own time. Although the tunnelers were instructed about the need for decompression before leaving the tunnel, nevertheless three men died from nitrogen embolism or 'the bends.'

Construction continued to advance at a good rate underground. On 23 August 1890, a hole was punched through the clay between the shields. It was claimed that the first freight through the tunnel was a plug of tobacco passed through this hole on the end of a shovel.

After passing through thousands of feet of clay, the two shields met almost exactly, off only a small fraction of an inch, on August 30th. The interior of the Canadian-built shield was then torn out and the outsides left in position to become tunnel walls where they remain in place to this day. The first man through the tunnel was the Canadian engineer, Sir Joseph Hobson. Freight service started 27 October 1891, and passenger service began on December 7th.

The opening of the St Clair Tunnel was celebrated in a proper style that reflected well on tradition. The first celebration, although not the official one, was touched off at noon on Sunday, 25 August 1891, when Hobson, who clearly had a flair for the dramatic, removed the last shovelful of dirt remaining between the US and Canadian diggers, and stepped through the opening. As he did, shrieking steam whistles on the surface gave the long-awaited signal that the first international underwater connection now existed.

The Port Huron *Daily Times* prepared an extensive edition to mark the opening, banquets were planned, and the entire area geared to the event. On Friday evening, September 18th, Port Huron held its banquet celebration with Canadian guests arriving from Point Edward aboard the steam passenger ferry, *Omar D Conger*. Among these was Sir Henry Tyler, Mayor Watson of Sarnia, and of course, Joseph Hobson. The most notable American present was Governor Vinans of Michigan. The dinner ended at an early hour so that the guests could return to Point Edward in time to prepare the extensive activities scheduled for the next day.

The following day a seven-coach inaugural train left Point Edward at 12:30 pm headed by a tall-stacked 4–4–0 type locomotive with a huge oil lantern atop the smoke box. It carried several flags and bunting and it was said to have been decorated with flowers as well.

At 1:00pm the train started for the tunnel entrance amid the cheers of the crowd, and three-and-a-half minutes after entering the Sarnia portal it emerged from the flag-draped stone portal on the US side as a grand orchestra of steam whistles greeted it, continuing to blow until the train passed through that exuberant archway. Then it rolled on on more decorous quiet to the new 22nd Street depot. A large freight house nearby was decorated with flags, bunting and evergreen boughs with a speaker's platform constructed on the east end and this was the next center of activity. Hobson received a tumultuous ovation which reportedly visibly affected him. The stay in Port Huron could not have lasted too long as tickets for the primary formal celebration showed that it was to begin at two o'clock that afternoon. And a grand affair it was with 350 people attending in the cavernous flag-draped Sarnia freight house.

As construction crews were inching through the heavy blue clay, orders were placed with the Baldwin Locomotive Works of Philadelphia for four of the largest engines yet built. Heavy steam power in the enclosed space of a tunnel posed a difficult problem for locomotive designers as did the steep gradients, but Baldwin's solutions were very logical and resulted in a locomotive dramatic in its appearance.

The major danger after the tunnel became operational was not compressed gases, but flue gases. The tunnel company took what they considered to be exceptional precautions by building a ventilation system with 'extraordinary capacity.' A *Scientific American* article published during the construction of the tunnel declaimed on how the redundant system would ensure that there were no problems with the air in the tunnel. But there were problems, nevertheless. A set of blowers and vents built throughout the tube could circulate 10,000 cubic feet of air a minute, but in practice, more time was needed since the air was removed somewhat irregularly. The first recorded casualty was Thomas Wright, a Port Huron mason who was overcome by smoke on 20 November 1897, but survived his dose of carbon monoxide, nitrous oxide, sulfur dioxide and other gases. Eight days later a coupling gave way on a twenty-car train working up the grade and several cars rolled back to the lowest point in the tunnel. Engineer PO Courtney, probably more concerned about the views of his superiors than his own safety and that of his crew, backed his locomotive down the tunnel to recouple the cars without waiting for the ventilation system to clear the fumes. It was a fatal mistake followed by still another: Courtney and his crew were overcome, and when his engine did not return another was dispatched. The crew of the rescue locomotive also was asphyxiated and both engines were trapped at the center of the tunnel, spewing out deadly gases. Courtney, the conductor and a brakeman died but the fireman recovered.

On 9 October 1904, a similar but even more tragic disaster took place. A livestock train eastbound and on the upgrade at Sarnia lost cars which, as before, rolled back to the lowest part of the tunnel. Tunnel crew engineer Joseph Simpson was in a caboose with the lost cars and was probably the first to die. When the remainder of the train emerged the crew, with vivid memories of the 1897 disaster in mind, had some sharp discussion on what they would do. One brakeman refused to go back, another returned in a later rescue attempt, but the engineer and fireman decided to enter the tunnel at once. The engineer died but the fireman put his head in a partially-filled fresh water tank and breathed the relatively pure air in the tank until rescued. Another rescue engine also went in from the Canadian side, and from the American end tunnel superintendent Alexander S Begg and two others along with a pumpman entered on foot. Begg collapsed and died before he reached the caboose. An engineer, Morden, collapsed as he tried to reach Begg but was later removed and he recovered. Three crewmen on the rescue locomotive also died in the deadly gases. The livestock, sheep and cattle, were all asphyxiated.

The tunnel engines, however, performed as anticipated with a limit of six trains per hour, hauling between twenty-five and thirty-three cars, with a total weight of no more than 760 tons at a speed of three miles per hour. With the opening of the tunnel, travel time to New York was cut by two hours and the Grand Trunk save a then-princely $50,000 a year by elimination of its ferries. Traffic soon exceeded expectations, however, and it became apparent that more frequent and longer trains were urgently needed to cope with the tonnages that had to pass through the single-track tunnel. By 1900 alternative motive power was being considered and by 1904 the Grand Trunk was seriously exploring electrification, a system then still in its infancy for running trains. Motivated by the tragedies in the tunnel, the railroad decided to operate it with electric locomotives.

The General Electric Company had aquired several contracts for DC (direct current) equipment but its competitor, Westinghouse, was anxious to secure a foothold in the railroad electrification field with its AC (alternating current) system. A combination of technical arguments and a favorable price won the day for Westinghouse and once more the tunnel was the site of extensive construction as eight heavy copper power lines were installed the length of the tube. A brick power house was built in Port Huron, furnished with two Westinghouse generators. Boilers, coal bunkers and a coal dock were also built on the river bank. Over nine miles of track were put under wires at a cost, by one estimate, of $500,000. Inside the tunnel, an additional 500 lights were installed, and the soot-begrimed walls were cleaned and painted white. All work was completed in 1908.

Once again, Grand Trunk and St Clair Tunnel Co officials turned to Baldwin for the new locomotives and once more Baldwin turned out sturdy specimens of utilitarian design. Not a trace of decoration appeared on the interior or exterior. These were large, slow three-axle engines that drew 3300 volts and reduced it to 300 volts for use at the motors. They were designed to provide enough power to start a 1000-ton train on the two percent grade. Thus the tunnel, with electrification and in particular AC electrification, a 'big project first' was back in the forefront of scientific and engineering news.

The initial electrified trip through the tunnel took place in February 1908 with a 700-ton train. All steam operations ended in May. On November 12, the Grand Trunk formally accepted the contractors' work and there was another celebration, not of the magnitude of the tunnel opening festivities but still a redoubtable one. A party of railroad officials, electrical engineers and members of the press were carried through the tunnel on a 'special.' They then adjourned to the Hotel Vendome in Sarnia to face the usual formidable dinners of the era and the even more formidable round of speeches by Grand Trunk officials, Westinghouse executives, other railroad men and doubtless, several local politicians.

Running time was reduced for the three-mile trip from 15 minutes for steam to 10 minutes while the tunnel's capacity was increased by about one-third. The St Clair Tunnel was the heaviest railroad service powered by electricity in the world.

More changes were in store and in 1917 the Detroit Edison Company was awarded a contract to supply electrical power and a new substation was built to furnish 50,000 watts to the locomotives and for the lights, ventilation system and drainage pumps. Boilers, generators and other equipment were torn out of the old generating plant. The coal bunkers were converted to storage bunkers. The nine electric locomotives were maintained in exceptional condition and served very well even though they accumulated enough years of service to have retired other locomotive types. When Westinghouse discontinued manufacturing replacement parts, the railroad acquired all of the jigs, mandrels and related equipment and in a Canadian shop were able to make any required replacement items.

The electrics were still functioning smoothly and effectively when they were finally retired in favor of diesels.

The beginning of the end came in the spring of 1957 when diesels were coupled at the head of passenger trains, although freights were still pulled by the electrics. Extensive tests indicated that the old problem of exhaust gas was too much to handle, although lighter passenger trains were able to drift well past the tunnel's mid-point, thus limiting the fumes. However, reviving the old ventilation system from steam days and augmenting it with new fans at the portals largely solved the problem. On 28 September 1958, the electrics were withdrawn ending the last electric main line railroad operation in Michigan and the last 'tunnel only' railroad electrification in the United States.

Today the colorful diesel locomotives of the Grand Trunk Western, Canadian National, Amtrak and VIA Rail move across the border through the tunnel and it seems quite possible that diesel motive power will be pulling trains under the river for the foreseeable future.

Because of its vital international importance as a transportation link, the St Clair Tunnel has been the target of two ill-fated sabotage attempts. As World War I began, an extraordinarily successful German sabotage ring operating out of the Imperial German Embassy in Washington, DC, was activated, headed by some daring naval attaches and diplomats amply supplied with cash, and said to be responsible for the great Black Tom explosion which destroyed a huge New Jersey powder factory.

Shortly after the main German thrust into France was halted, the attention of the saboteurs turned to the main communications arteries between Canada, which was in the war, and the United States, still neutral but selling war material to Canada. Several bridges were targeted as was the Port Huron-Sarnia tunnel and the Detroit River railroad tunnel. One operation involving local people was identified: Altert Kaltshmidt of Detroit, president of the Marine City Salt Company, was said to have been in charge of sabotage operations for the German government over most of the northern United States and central Canada. Kaltschmidt hired four agents, presumably familiar with explosives, and sent them to blow up a bridge in western Canada. They abandoned this project and he next assigned them to the St Clair Tunnel. They checked and reported back that the tunnel couldn't be easily wrecked, and that the scheme should be forgotten. Kaltschmidt told them to proceed anyhow.

Working in Kaltshmidt's home was a young girl who could understand German. She overheard the plotters, gained some knowledge of what they were planning and reported these plans to nearby authorities who told her to stay on the job and learn whatever else she could. She subsequently heard that the plotters had decided to send a carload of dynamite through the tunnel with a timer set to explode when the car reached center. The authorities moved in and some 50 people were detained and arrested. The tunnel was heavily guarded for the rest of the war.

In 1940 another attempt to sabotage the tunnel was made. In June of that year a fire was discovered in a freight car headed from Port Huron to Sarnia. Holes had been bored in the car's floor, oil-soaked rags inserted and ignited. The fire was extinguished with only modest damage. Railroad detectives, the Royal Canadian Mounted Police, the St Clair County sheriff's office and

Above: A Grand Trunk Western doubleheader emerges from beneath the St Clair River; electricity eventually gave way to diesel, and nearly 100 years after its opening, the St Clair Tunnel continues to serve international rail traffic. The tunnel's smallness, however, is a problem.

the Michigan State Police mounted a massive investigation which turned up no culprits but arrived at an interesting conclusion: they believed the arsonists intended to hit a carload of munitions that had, fortunately, been moved across the previous day. Had an explosion occurred it could have closed the tunnel and possibly severely damaged the large Imperial Oil refinery located near the Canadian entrance.

The whole tunnel system was carefully guarded thereafter with round-the-clock squads of home guards at strategic places. In spite of German agents and human fallibility, the 1904 tragedy was the last involving life and limb and, with a few short closures, the tunnel has been available for service almost continuously ever since.

Today, the 96 year-old tunnel has settled into a respectable and serviceable old age. At this time it looks as though the St Clair Tunnel will make its centennial anniversary still useful and an important part of North American rail transportation. The main threat now come from its size, a problem that has plagued it for almost fifty years. In the 1930s and 1940s freight cars were getting larger and some cars could not be sent through the tube although when the tunnel was built planners allowed good margins for growth. In 1946, a low roadbed was laid dropping the rail seven inches. It was announced that year that all equipment could now be routed through, but that seven inches was not enough as cars were built with ever increasing dimensions, particularly automobile carriers.

In 1971, the Canadian National system returned car ferries to the St Clair River to handle the auto carriers and other oversize cars. If freight cars continue to expand in size and as older cars are retired, the historic tube may become obsolete. On the other hand, it is possible that new and changing traffic patterns could produce a trend toward more compact cars, particularly given the recent enormous growth of small high-tech industries with small tonnage shipping requirements. Moreover, pressures for coal and ore slurry pipelines may mean that railroads will again have to compete for the smaller shipper, with lesser volume needs per car. If so, the tunnel could be a commercial success for the foreseeable future.

Since the opening days, international passenger trains running from Toronto to Chicago have been an integral part of tunnel operations. In 1971, the service through the tunnel ended. Amtrak re-established international service on 31 October 1982, running a train daily each way between Chicago and Toronto via Port Huron. Despite limited promotion, reports are that patronage is reasonably good.

There are some 'ifs' in the picture but from a current perspective it looks as though this engineering marvel will serve for many years to come.

Canada's Railways Enter the 20th Century

The Turn of the Century and World War I

At the turn of our century, Canadians were very optimistic about the future. Many people believed this would soon become one the greatest nations in the world. Prime Minister Sir Wilfrid Laurier said, 'The 20th century belongs to Canada.'

But the young land needed more people, to open up the wilderness and establish industries. The government began advertising to attract immigrants, with huge posters displayed all over England and in Europe's major cities. They described the rich farmlands and wonderful opportunities to be found in Canada. The campaign worked; thousands upon thousands of immigrants began pouring into Canada, many of them heading for the West. More and still more new rail lines were needed in the West. Canadian Pacific could not keep up with the demand.

'Railway mania' held Canadians in thrall for decades. Railways and their progress were a constant major topic of conversation across the country; newspapers were full of stories about them. The government led by Sir Wilfrid Laurier in 1903 began generously handing out loans or guaranteeing bonds to build, build, build! Money also poured in from investors in Britain.

Between 1870 and 1900, rail travel became much more comfortable. In fact, some of the passenger trains became quite elegant. On the outside, coaches were beautifully painted in bright colours. Inside, first-class parlour cars had wood carvings on the ceilings, and paintings displayed on mahogany-panelled walls. Plush carpets were laid, and at windows hung draperies of rich fabrics. By 1888, certain trains had coaches lighted by electricity and heated by steam. Some cars even boasted a primitive form of air-conditioning: fans blowing across blocks of ice. Dining cars offered six-course meals, served in the style of fine hotels.

At right and above right: These 4–6–0s provided northern rail speed at the turn of the century. At that time, some railroads 'farther south' were doing well with 4–4–2 Atlantics and, eventually, 4–6–2 Pacifics.

The railways made many other, practical improvements, too. Iron rails were replaced by steel which took much longer to wear out, and major wooden bridges were replaced with iron. As wood-burning locomotives were replaced with by ones using coal, trains could travel longer distances without stopping to refuel.

In just 50 years, Canada's railways had made amazing progress—from 80 miles of trackage in 1850 to 16,950 in 1900—and the country grew along with them.

When the pace of construction slackened in 1914, Canada had achieved a remarkable position in the railway world. Only five other countries—the United States, Russia, Germany, India and France—possessed a greater mileage, and relative to population none came anywhere near her. Three great systems stretched from coast to coast. Need still existed for local extensions, but by great effort the main trunk lines had been built. Not only in mileage were the railways of Canada notable. In the degree to which the minor roads had been swallowed up by a few dominating systems, in the wide sweep of their outside operations, in their extension beyond the borders of Canada itself, and in the degree to which they had been built by public aid, they challenged attention.

While there were nearly 90 railway companies in Canada in 1914, the three trancontinental systems—the Canadian Northern, the Canadian Pacific and the Grand Trunk—controlled more than 80 percent of the total mileage and also owned a variety of subsidiary undertakings such as steamships, hotels, express service, irrigation and land development and grain elevators. The control by Canadian railways of seven or eight thousand miles of lines in the United States, with corresponding extensions into Canada by American lines, was an outcome of geographic conditions, intimate social and trade connections, and a civilized view of international relations which no other countries could match.

However, since the companies doing the building were privately owned, they owed it to their shareholders to follow the shortest routes to major ports and centres of population, because that was how profits would be made. This didn't always serve the nation's future interests. Geography, climate, and patterns of settlement in Canada and the United States favoured north-south traffic, and the Grand Trunk, for example, preferred the year-round harbor at Portland, Maine, to any port in Atlantic Canada.

Opposition Leader Robert L Borden began arguing for a Canadian line, owned by the Canadian people, through Canadian people, through Canadian territory, to Canadian ports.

In 1915, the CPR already had a system running from Saint John, New Brunswick, to the West Coast. Now the National Transcontinental, the Canadian Northern, and the Grand Trunk Pacific began cross-country operations. The nation had a fantastic 34,915 miles of trackage.

When the First World War began in 1914, British money was needed at home to train and equip an army, and there was none to spare for loans to Canada's railways. The flow of immigrants to Canada from Europe also stopped, but industrial and commercial development flourished across the land.

Locomotives and facilities were very important as the 20th century dawned— high hopes for Canada's future made the railroading picture doubly bright. Such facilities as this roundhouse, shown *at right* during its construction at Durand, Michigan in 1912, made yard work easier.

Left: This Canadian National 4–6–0 was built at Montreal in 1913, and is shown here at the Vancouver, BC Steam Expo on 22 May 1986. This loco is almost as tall as a two-story house, and its high, narrow stack identifies it as a coal burner. *Above:* A period photo of CN Chairman DB Hanna.

It was the patriotic duty of Canada's railways to carry men and matériel from as far as the West coast to eastern ports, where ships waited to take them to England. However, the government paid unremunerative rates for their efforts. Within a couple of years all the companies except Canadian Pacific were deep in debt.

The Creation of Canadian National

Sir Robert Borden, who had become prime minister in 1911, kept arguing for public ownership of a nationwide railway system. He pointed out that 90 percent of the Grand Trunk's transcontinental ambitions were already publicly funded by government loans, and for only 10 percent more the country could own and control the system. Faced by the urgent demands of the war, Parliament decided to act on his suggestion.

It began in 1917 by obtaining the Canadian Northern and appointing a board of directors chaired by DB Hanna. The following year, the board's jurisdiction was extended over the Canadian Government Railways, 15 lines in all, the main ones being the Intercolonial, the National Transcontinental, the Hudson Bay Railway, and the Prince Edward Island Railway.

Then, on 6 June 1919, Parliament passed an Act incorporating the Canadian National Railway Company and appointed Hanna as president. The first major acquisition made by the new corporation was of the Grand Trunk Pacific the following year.

The first annual report issued by the board of directors was for 1921, the third year in the life of the National System.' They gave details of the assets and liabilities of the component companies as well as those of Canadian National. They reported net earnings in 1921 of

$47,321.44, compared with a 1920 deficit of $4 million. Then they went on with their work of assembly. By 1923, with the takeover of the Grand Trunk Railway, they had laid a solid foundation.

When the Government of Canada incorporated Canadian National, it created one of the largest railways in the world, with various railway-related services operated for the benefit of its sole shareholder, the people of Canada. It had 105,905 employees and 2078 pensioners. From the many companies assembled in it came 3268 locomotives pulling 138,925 cars of various types along more than 21,700 miles of track, and also telegraph lines, hotels, steamships, car ferries, barges and tugs.

Canadian National Telegraphs had 3852 employees serving the railway and the public by sending messages along 113,105 miles of wire. The Express Department had 3255 employees, as well as '628 horses, 111 motor trucks, 1095 waggons and sleighs, 2959 platform trucks and sleighs, and 584 safes.' Among the business handled during the year were 47 million pounds of fish, 3500 live foxes and 4400 'Horses, principally race horses.'

Eight major hotels, built by some of the companies which made up 'the CNR' to provide their passengers with first-class places to stay as they travelled, were not operated by a separate department but rather entrusted to a 'General Manager, Hotels and Sleeping and Dining Cars.'

Above: An early 20th century CN 4–6–4 Hudson passenger loco. *At right:* A somewhat later CN 4–8–4 Northern freight loco. Note these locomotives' short stacks and heavy tank tenders. *Below:* This coal burning 2–8–2 CN Mikado class loco is similar to the larger 2–10–2 'Santa Fe' class locomotives.

Above: These hopeful-looking folks were part of the huge Hungarian immigrant influx of 1926. *Below left:* An elegant, powerful CN passenger engine leads its train at Shawinigan, Quebec. This photo was taken in 1970, during an exhibition run. Regular Canadian steam service ended years earlier. *Above left:* The CN's Saskatoon freight yard in the 1930s.

Although the basic groundwork of consolidation had been completed by 1923, a great deal of fine tuning remained to be done, and it took many more years. The timetables, work rules, salaries and services originated by different companies had to be adjusted to conform across the country. Many of the lines assembled in the CNR had been built close together to compete for traffic in the same areas, and much of the track belonging to smaller and poorer railways was in sorry condition. Decisions had to be made regarding which lines were worth repairing and which should be kept. Many of the lines had been built close together to compete for traffic in the same area. These extra lines were no longer needed. Much of the track belonging to the smaller and poorer railways was in bad shape. Men who had worked in fierce competition with one another now had to learn to work together. At first, it was hard for them to forget their loyalty to the old companies.

The CNR's first president, DB Hanna had been a vice-president of the Canadian Northern. When the Canadian Government gave him the huge job of pulling the new company together it made an excellent choice.

The next president, Sir Henry Thornton, appointed in 1922, was an American businessman known on two continents.

In 1923, Sir Henry established the first radio network in Canada, to entertain the CNR's passengers. Special railway cars were equipped with receivers, and headsets through which travellers could hear programs broadcast by the station in the vicinity of the train. There were stations in eight cities, their call letters all beginning with 'CNR', for example CNRM in Montreal and CNRE in Edmonton. In the 1930s, this network became a separate company, the forerunner of today's Canadian Broadcasting Corporation.

To attract new immigrants to settle near the railway's lines, Sir Henry created a special service which helped them find jobs and adjust to their new environment.

In addition to helping grain farmers by shipping their wheat to market, the railway each fall ran special 'harvest trains' that carried hundreds of young men from Eastern Canada out to the West to help bring in the crops. At each stop on the Prairies, farmers waited to pick out strong-looking workers and offer them jobs.

Perhaps the most unusual special trains of the 1920s were those that carried raw silk. It was shipped in huge quantities from Japan to New York City to be processed and woven into beautiful, expensive cloth. Because the raw silk rotted very quickly if it was not processed within a few days, speed was essential in its transportation. Some

of the fastest ships in the world were used to carry it from Japan to Vancouver, where it was loaded into trains in less than 30 minutes, and then, as the trains sped across the country, all other traffic halted to give them the right of way. With essential stops for fuel and water lasting only 10 minutes each, the entire journey across North America took only 80 hours.

After the Canada-West Indies Trade Agreement was signed in the mid-1920s, the government asked the CNR to establish a fleet of passenger ships. Seven luxury liners flew the company's marine pennant for the next few decades, from Montreal, Halifax, and Saint John to the Caribbean, until competition from airlines became too great.

One of the railway's most important tasks during the 1920s was moving Canadian grain from the Prairies to seaports on both coasts. In 1929, a new direction was inaugurated, to Churchill on Hudson Bay. However, although it took less time for ships to reach Europe from Churchill, the port at what is now called Thunder Bay (known then as the twin cities of Fort William and Port

Arthur) remained the major grain-handling position of central Canada because it had more ice-free weeks each year.

Troubles: The Great Depression and World War II

The Great Depression of the 1930s meant hard times around the world. Industries, struggling to survive, produced fewer goods for railways to ship. And then came long years of drought on Canada's prairies, during which grain traffic fell off drastically.

Few people earned enough to be able to pay for train tickets, but thousands began to travel about the country in search of jobs. Always hoping to find work, spurred on by countless rumours as to where it might be found, scores of wandering men hid in empty box cars to ride to yet another city. Or, when the weather was good, they simply lay on the roofs of cars, risking their lives out of sheer desperation.

Although it touched every aspect of Canadian life, in many cases hindering or even obliterating the natural course of development, the Depression did not stop progress in technology.

During the 1930s, aircraft—not only planes but hydrogen-filled dirigibles—became sophisticated enough to carry passengers, mail and cargo on regular schedules. The Canadian Government decided a national airline was needed, and in 1937 Trans-Canada Air Lines was incorporated, but as part of the CNR because its officers had the transportation experience required to get the new venture started. The then president of the railway, SJ Hungerford, was appointed as first president of TCA. Thus in its formative years the airline known as Air Canada was, like the CBC, guided by the Canadian National.

Just as the Depression ended, much of the world went to war again and from 1939 to 1945 Canada's railways were involved in an all-out effort. Tanks, guns, planes, ammunition, supplies, food, and men all had to be

Below: These unfortunates were photographed in the midst of a Depression-era resettlement from Montreal to Lois, Quebec. Folks with money enough for tickets travelled far for work; others 'hopped freights.'

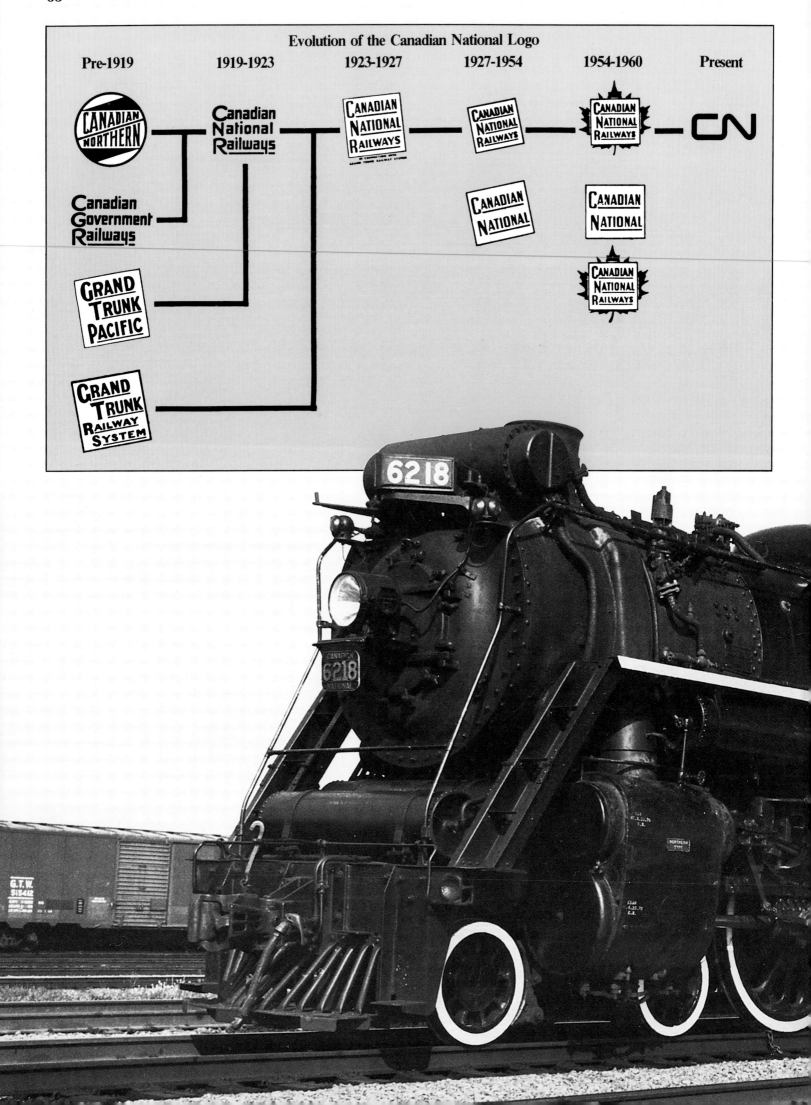

Evolution of the Canadian National Logo

| Pre-1919 | 1919-1923 | 1923-1927 | 1927-1954 | 1954-1960 | Present |

The last Canadian National steam locomotive in regular service was CN loco number 6218, a 4–8–4 Northern class oil burner, which is shown *below* on a siding in a CN yard, where it is kept in good condition for exhibition runs. *Above:* Number 6400 was a very hot-looking 4-8-4 streamliner of the early 1940s, complete with ride-smoothing 12-wheel tender.

transported to the East Coast, where ships waited to take them to Europe. Because troops and matériel took precedence over passengers, schedules for the travelling public became chaotic.

Canadian National's traffic doubled so quickly that the company did not have enough equipment to handle it. Old box cars and passenger cars were taken out of retirement and rebuilt. Some of the company's work shops, normally used to repair cars and locomotives, also served as munitions factories. Because more than 20,000 men of the CNR served in the war, much of the hard work that kept the railway going was done by women.

Wars, inevitably, are the pivotal experiences for the nations involved in them. While a war is in progress, nothing can possibly be normal; when it ends 'normal' means completely different things than it did before. After a war, one can truly say that 'Nothing is the way it used to be.'

During the Second World War, Canadian National was unable to buy new rolling stock because none was being built (steel went into war-related products), so the cars it did have were used to their limits. When the war ended, the company needed a great deal of money to replace worn-out equipment.

There was also a new challenge railways had never encountered before: good highways had been built right across the country, and people had acquired the habit of using other vehicles instead of trains. Driving a car meant having the freedom to travel when and where you pleased. Trucks offered door-to-door freight services, taking a lot of business away from railways. And airplanes were becoming popular with travellers in a hurry.

Some people said railways weren't needed any more because the world had encountered a new age in which they would be replaced forever by other modes of transportation. Stiff competition for traffic was the toughest challenge railways had ever had to face, and if they could not find ways to compete, it really would mean the end.

The man asked by the Canadian government in 1950 to take up this challenge at the CNR was Donald Gordon, a strong, able leader who had chaired the Wartime Prices and Trade Board. He, along with many other people, believed railways were still very important and would continue to be so.

As president, Mr Gordon immediately set about pulling the company back into shape. To replace the old, worn-out cars, he ordered new specialized ones which shippers liked because they were easier to load and unload, and could carry more freight. Also, over a period of some ten years, he brought an entire fleet of new diesel-electric locomotives which were much less expensive to operate and maintain than steam locomotives.

Along with new equipment and improved methods of operating came a new way of thinking. Before this, trains were the only choice passengers and shippers had; railways could offer the kind of service they chose to provide because traffic had to come to them anyway. Faced by competition from other modes, Canadian National realized it would have to offer its customers the service that best suited *them*. Only be serving people's needs better than other modes of transport would the company pay its way.

At left: The CN's Prince Rupert, BC Ticket Office in the mid-1930s.

These pages: Hauling a train of grain cars, vintage CN locomotive number 6060 arrives at Boston Bar en route to Vancouver for the Steam Expo there in 1986. Note the unusual use of two 12-wheel tenders coupled to this semi-streamlined 2–8–2 Mikado class engine. The age of diesels made engines such as this classic locomotive obsolete.

CN Today

A New Era

Canadian National is today a public utility whose activities, in one way or another, touch regularly the day-to-day lives of most Canadians. In addition to the movement of people and products by rail, it operates trucking lines, a coast-to-coast chain of hotels, an extensive telecommunications network, a fleet of coastal ships, and a variety of related services in such fields as industrial location, customer research, physical distribution, real estate and urban renewal. Through its wholly owned United States subsidiaries, most notably the Grand Trunk Western Railroad, CN's operations reach into 12 of the American states. CN had always had links with Europe, but today it also has offices or agents in Australia, China, Hong Kong, Japan, Korea, Malaysia and Taiwan. The development of CN into the advanced system we know today took some time and hard work.

Most of the track built before the 1920s ran across Canada from east to west to bind the nation together. Now, to find new traffic, the CNR began building lines to the north, to transport ore from areas where minerals had been discovered. Hauling many tons of raw materials over long distances is a job railways do best, and most of the new lines were very profitable. The longest one, the Great Slave Lake Railway, stretches from northern Alberta into the Northwest Territories.

To compete with airlines and trucking companies, new technology and equipment and working methods were introduced on the railway to make service faster and less expensive.

As the railway was modernized, so too were the services which had grown up around it. During the 1970s, departments such as hotels and telecommunications became separate profit centers, and the pattern of a diver-

At right: Two SD40–2 road switchers sandwich an Alco C–630 in a 9000hp freight train crossing Montreal's Victoria Bridge. *Above right:* A Canadian National passenger train speeds along a causeway through beautiful countryside, in CN's passenger train days—before VIA Rail.

Above: Here represented sequentially, from right to left, is the history—from steam to diesel—of CN locomotives. *Left:* Five 3000-horsepower EMD SD40-2s haul a CN iron ore train through wintertime Ontario. *Above right:* This CN Electro Motive F7 diesel developed 1500hp, and was but a harbinger of more sophisticated diesel locomotives to come.

sified corporation with interactive, mutually supportive parts emerged.

One can scarcely imagine a business more sensitive to change than a railway. Its fortunes can be suddenly and adversely affected by anything from the spring flooding of an obscure river to a shift in political alliances among nations or a drop in the world price of potash. And all the activities surrounding a railway are exceptionally vulnerable as well, to external forces ranging from new technology to public taste.

The way Canadians use their railways never stops changing. In 1977, the passenger services of both CN and Canadian Pacific were entrusted to a new Crown corporation, VIA Rail. Since the Second World War, many freight customers relocated from the center of cities, railway lands were freed for new uses and urban renewal blossomed.

CN Real Estate was set up to develop the railway's lands in the hearts of Canada's major cities by building major office complexes and underground shopping malls. Other railway lands, in the West, were found to be rich in oil and gas, and CN Exploration Inc has many wells in production.

CNR Telegraphs grew into a subsidiary company, CN Communications, which operates NorthWesTel in the

Yukon and northern British Columbia, and Terra Nova Tel in Newfoundland, and, in partnership with Canadian Pacific, runs the giant CNCP Telecommunications system and Telecommunications Terminal Systems. CN Communications leases space in The CN Tower to CNCP Telecommunications and other companies which provide the Metro Toronto area with 'ghost-free' television, radio, and mobile radio systems.

The Business End

CN today is one of the largest Canadian corporations, with most of its $5 billion in assets devoted to transportation.

Private companies have shareholders who elect a board of directors. In CN's case, the shareholders are the people of Canada and the federal government appoints CN's board of directors. This means that each Canadian owns a part of CN.

Each year, a portion of the profit made by CN is paid to the federal treasury, as a dividend for the people of Canada.

As in most corporations, CN is organized into divisions which carry on the various activities in the railway, trucking, hotels, telecommunications and other fields. The main divisions are CN Rail, Grand Trunk Corporation, CN Communications, CN Trucking, CN Express, CN Hotels and Tower, CN Marine and Terra Transport.Not surprisingly, CN's broad-ranging experience in transportation, communications, and related fields resulted in the establishment of Canac International Inc, the domestic and

international consulting arm of Canadian National. This business unit assembles teams of specialists, as required, from other parts of CN to work on contract for private enterprises or governments in Canada and around the world.

The Railway

The railway arm of Canadian National is called CN Rail and its performance as a freight-hauling railway is very good. The rail operation of today is not the same as it was years ago. For example, productivity gains obtained through computerization and modernization have enabled CN Rail to double the traffic carried while cutting the work force in half.

To get an idea of the size of the railway, we need only consider the earnings of $6 million a day from hauling such items as resource products, manufactured goods and processed foods.

This requires a fleet of 2200 diesel-electric locomotives and about 92,000 railway cars of all types. There are 24,950 miles of main railway line operated by CN Rail, making it one of the longest railways in the world.

CN Rail's status as one of the largest and most successful railways in North America came about in part because of its efforts to introduce and follow through on innovations. In one of its boldest moves, it enlarged upon a new way of handling cargo, called the intermodal concept. Each type of transportation, whether truck, train or ship, is called a mode. When two or more modes are used together it is referred to as intermodal.

Freight is the modern CN's mainstay, and improvements in this area of burdenage include the use of laser beams *(upper left)* in freight yards to identify cars and cargo for more efficient car placement and routing; specialized carriers such as the high-capacity grain cars at *lower left*; and cargo specialty diversification, as is evidenced by the long sulfur 'unit' train shown *above*. Unit trains are comprised of semi-permanently coupled cars.

This can take the form of containers, huge metal or plywood boxes which carry most types of merchandise, loaded on a ship overseas. On arrival in Canada, the containers are later taken off the ships and placed on railway flat cars which are then hauled in special trains to their final destination. In those cities, the containers are taken off the flat cars and placed on small flat-bed trucks and driven to factories or business locations.

Other forms of intermodal travel include piggybacking of highway trailers on railway flat cars, to reduce truck miles and fuel consumption, and Cargo-Flo, in which liquid and liquidized forms of a wide variety of raw materials can be pumped from a railway tank car to a tanker truck for local hauling purposes.

CN Rail also works with water transportation in other ways. Coal, potash, grain and a multitude of other bulk products can be carried by train to bulk storage facilities on the Great Lakes and on either coast of Canada. The bulk storage bins can then be emptied into ocean-going vessels and lake carriers for transportation to user industries in North America or around the world.

On the west coast, east coast and St Lawrence River, another system enables railway cars to be carried on ferry boats and barges. The vessels have actual railway tracks fastened to the deck and the railway cars roll on those tracks.

Symbolic of CN vitality is this freight train. shown *above*. coming head-on over the rails near Snider. Ontario. *Right:* Another CN freight 'makes book' amid the sunset wilds of Fraser Canyon. British Columbia.

The most unusual application is on the east coast where rail ferries operate between North Sydney, Nova Scotia, and Port aux Basques, Newfoundland. The railway line operated by Terra Transport, the division which controls CN's transportation activities in Newfoundland, is a narrow-gauge line. This means that the distance between the two rails is narrower than on CN Rail lines.

To accommodate this change in track width, a special shop in Port aux Basques lifts the box cars, removes the mainland-width wheel assemblies and installs Newfoundland-width wheel assemblies.

The emphasis on maintenance pervades CN Rail's operating philosophy. Money spent permits continuing and efficient use of existing rolling stock and rail facilities. That is why the basic tools of the system—roadbed, rails and rolling stock—are constantly being upgraded and maintained.

CN Rail's main line across Canada has been dramatically improved with continuously welded rail, upgraded roadbed, extended sidings and new automatic central traffic control equipment. Some of the latest mechanized equipment is being used to carry out this work.

Maintenance of the rolling stock and locomotives is carried out on a regular basis to avoid premature wear and failures in service. To increase the car life of its existing fleet, CN Rail conducts an ongoing repair program which results in the overhaul of some 6000 freight cars annually.

These pages: Two heavy road switchers pull a Canadian National grain and freight train along and over the Thompson River in British Columbia. The long train is indicative of the health of the CN's freight business, as is the well-kept rolling stock of which this train is comprised.

The purchase of new rolling stock is still made on a regular basis. However, the demand for new cars is actually decreasing because computer technology and better car management have resulted in faster turnaround of railway cars. This means the same number of cars can now handle more traffic. Improvements in locomotive traction have also meant that fewer locomotoves are needed to have the same number of cars.

Where maintenance alone is not sufficient, CN Rail does not hesitate to adopt or develop new technology to meet its needs. Many of the innovations that have produced savings or efficiencies have been developed at CN Rail's own technical research center. Some examples: a CN Rail locomotive mini-computer that detects wheel slippage and automatically reduces power to the traction motors; self-steering freight cars which significantly reduce friction of car wheels against rail on curved sections of track; and the world's most advanced locomotive simulator, developed by CN Rail engineers. Used for training locomotive engineers, it is a full-size cab that does everything an operating locomotive does—except ride the rails.

Above: This 'Draper taper' locomotive has a cutaway behind the cab to give the engineer a view to the rear. The broad front of the loco *(at right)* is due to its 'safety cab' and 'cowl'. *At top:* A CN boxcar train.

A source of special pride to CN is the development of a new type of locomotive, the Draper Taper, with many advantages in safety and design. The new locomotive, given its name by Bombadier Inc, builders of the first production run, is in large measure the brainchild of W L 'Bill' Draper, assistant chief of motive power for the railway's operations department.

The locomotive, a mainline freight-haul unit, is of a wide car-body design, but features a revolutionary cutaway behind the cab. It is the cutaway which gives rise to the 'Draper Taper' nickname. It permits the engineer exceptional rear visibility for a wide car-body, and allows full-view inspection of the train, even on a very slight curve. The new locomotive also incorporates a number of other design features which should improve reliability of train operations, particularly in cold weather and heavy snow conditions. The combination of features built into 'Draper Taper' locomotives have become standard for all CN mainline freight-haul locomotives.

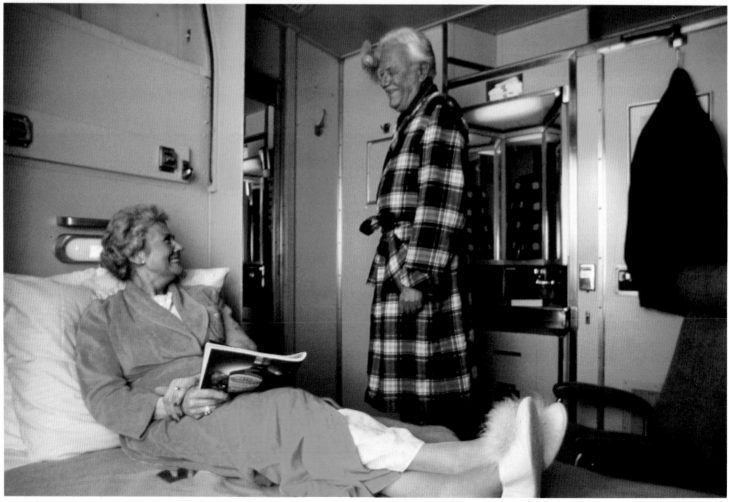

Above: A 1750hp EMD FP9 diesel hauls yet another VIA Rail train through the beauteous Canadian countryside. *Above left,* vacationers make their plans comfortably in a regular coach car; *at lower left,* mom and pop relax in their VIA sleeper; and *at right,* fun with mommy in a warmly-colored 'Daynighter' car. VIA Rail provides a full range of excellent passenger services, and runs schedules using such classic rail service as the *Canadian.*

VIA Rail Just for Passengers

CN has been a staunch supporter of passenger train travel and has introduced many on-train features that were copied elsewhere in North America.

By the time Canadian National was created there were two main routes—the traditional CP one and the new CN one—the Continental Ltd: Montréal to Vancouver via North Bay and Cochrane. The National, the Toronto section, joined the Continental at Winnepeg for the trip to the Pacific coast.

Various trains operated over these routes—names such as the Trans Canada Ltd, the Vancouver Express, The Dominion and the Coast Express come to mind. Some featured a choice of accommodations, ranging from deluxe bedrooms and dining cars to coaches and special 'Colonist' cars for immigrants heading west to homestead. Some were sleeping-car-only limited expresses.

In the 1950s, both CN and CP launched their ultra-modern transcontinental services, the Canadian and the Super Continental. Both these services were launched the same day, 24 April 1955. Both offered passengers the latest in travel comfort.

Both railways had just taken delivery of large orders of new cars. However, CP's train captured the limelight with its stainless-steel cars and sleek looks. The Canadian fea-

VIA's revolutionary Light, Rapid, Comfortable (LRC) service began in the early 1980s. Cars *(above)* and locos *(at top)* were designed for high speed operation—up to 125 mph—but haven't yet got all the bugs worked out. *At right:* VIA Rail's luxurious passenger train, the *Canadian,* tours the beautiful Rockies with its cars full of delighted passengers.

tured our country's fauna and flora in its decoration, hence its name. CN's Super Continental was pulled by twin gold and green diesels and featured pastel colours in its day coaches and parlour cars. It took its name from the Continental Ltd, which continued to run until 1964 when it was replaced by the Panorama.

But continuing losses made the passenger operation a financial drain on the railway. To remove this burden, the federal government created VIA Rail Canada, a separate Crown corporation. VIA entered into contracts with CN Rail and CP Rail for the use of rail lines and operating personnel for intercity trains across Canada. CN Rail is continuing to contribute to passenger train comfort because it has major contracts for repairing and maintaining VIA's passenger car fleet and also makes roadbed improvements.

The Super Continental, discontinued in 1981, resumed service 18 June 1985. It offered passengers the latest in travel comforts and its attractiveness provided a spur to tourism in Canada as it aroused a great deal of interest in trancontinental travel, both at home and abroad. The equipment ordered for this train is still being operated by VIA Rail Canada Inc 30 years later.

Lines in the US

CN Rail has direct ties with the United States through the Grand Trunk Western which connects with CN Rail at

Sarnia and Detroit, through the Duluth, Winnepeg and Pacific Railway which connects to the Winnipeg-Thunder Bay railway line, through Central Vermont which meets CN Rail at St Alban's, Vermont, and the Grand Trunk New England line which connects at Island Pond, Vermont. All of these subsidiaries are part of Grand Trunk Corporation, a holding company established by CN in 1971.

Grand Trunk Western is by far the largest and most important American railroad owned by Canadian National. Its 1311 miles of trackage connect Canada with some of the major industrial centres in the United States—Detroit, Toledo, Chicago, and Cincinnati. The history of the company began in the 1850s, when the Grand Trunk Railway of Canada decided to expand into the rich and growing Midwest of the United States. The first step was the construction in 1858 of a short railway with a very long name: the Chicago, Detroit and Canada Grand Trunk Junction Railway.

Others followed, and by the 1870s the Grand Trunk's directors realized they needed a line of their own to Chicago.

Above: This modern Grand Trunk Western freight seems to issue forth from the gleaming modernity of Detroit's Renaissance Center, towering in the background. The Central Vermont train shown *above right* is passing the CV's historic headquarters in St Albans, Vermont.

Two events in June 1878 convinced British managers of the Grand Trunk they would have to fight to survive in the American marketplace. Need for their own line to Chicago became a critical issue on 21 June 1878. On that date, William H Vanderbilt, son of Commodore Cornelius Vanderbilt and heir to the Commodore's $100 million New York Central empire, seized control of the Michigan Central Railroad in a Detroit stock vote. This action exposed Grand Trunk traffic moving between Detroit and Chicago to exorbitant rates imposed by Michigan Central.

Three days later, Vanderbilt unveiled another surprise. He sent a locomotive to blockade the Chicago and Lake Huron connection at Flint to deny Grand Trunk use of that line to Chicago. In dramatic fashion, Vanderbilt let the world know that he was the true owner of the Lansing-Flint 49-mile Chicago and North Eastern virtually in the middle of Chicago and Lake Huron trackage. Un-

known to the Chicago and Lake Huron owners, Vanderbilt had earlier bought $1.2 million of Chicago and North Eastern bonds in a secret deal with James M Turner, the C&NE president. Believing they controlled the Lansing-Flint connection, the surprised Chicago and Lake Huron owners discovered too late that the little Chicago and North Eastern in their midst had suddenly become a Vanderbilt viper and nearly as deadly.

Grand Trunk had little choice but to meet the rail rates imposed by Vanderbilt on the movement of its traffic. But, Grand Trunk's President Sir Henry Tyler and General Manager Joseph Hickson prepared counter-action to break the strangle-hold.

Six month after the uneasy truce set in between Grand Trunk and Vanderbilt, Hickson met secretly in Montreal with disgruntled Chicago and Lake Huron bondholders. He agreed to purchase their line. In May 1879, Sir Henry Tyler arrived in the United Sates from London and joined Hickson for a round of meetings with railroad executives and financiers.

Although Grand Trunk's interest in the Chicago and Lake Huron was rumored, Tyler and Hickson talked about various Chicago routes and met with so many different railroad people that no one was sure of their plans.

During their whirlwind inspection tour, they rode a special Chicago and Lake Huron train from Wellsboro, Indiana to Lansing, Michigan on 5 June. Despite lengthy stops at South Bend, Cassopolis, and Battle Creek, and 12 stops for grade crossings and orders, they completed the 115-mile trip to Lansing averaging better than 40 mph. They were greeted by the mayor of Lansing and Michigan Governor Charles M Croswell before traveling to Port Huron.

On 21 June 1879, Hickson's secret December negotiations with Chicago and Lake Huron bondholders brought results. At a Detroit auction, in which Grand Trunk was the only bidder, the Port Huron-Flint section of the Chicago and Lake Huron was purchased for $300,000. A few weeks later, Grand Trunk announced bids to build its own line between Lansing and Flint by way of Corunna and Owosso.

Realizing he had been outmaneuvered, William Vanderbilt offered to sell his Lansing-Flint (Chicago and North Eastern Railroad) property to Grand Trunk. He wanted

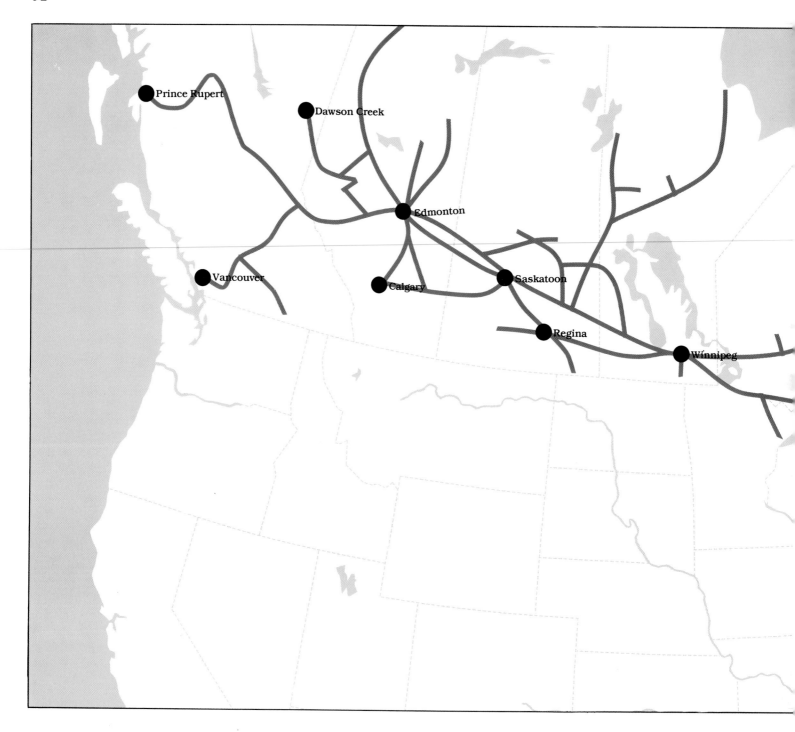

$600,000 or half the price he had paid in his secret deal to gain control. By 25 August Grand Trunk's Hickson had purchased the western section of the Chicago and Lake Huron (from Lansing to the Indiana boundary; 108 miles). This move totally isolated Vanderbilt's Lansing-Flint line. On September 3, he capitulated and sold the line to Grand Trunk for $540,000.

In London, England at the October 30 meeting of Grand Trunk Shareholder, Sir Henry Tyler said, 'The acquisition of this line to Chicago is, perhaps the most important event that has happened in the history of Grand Trunk.'

Twenty years after its formation, the Chicago and Grand Trunk Railway suffered financial difficulties and was reorganized on 22 November 1900 as Grand Trunk Western Railway.

In Canada, government officials and politicians viewed the activities and operations of railroads more closely than ever before. Railroad financial problems and overbuilding of lines demanded attention. Then, came World War I, the government's emergency use of railroads, the rise of nationalism, and serious talk of nationalizing Canadian railroads. Because of its size, the Grand Trunk Railway Company of Canada became a prime target.

Despite a desperate and bitter fight by Grand Trunk shareholders, the proud company was nationalized with other Canadian roads by passage of the Canadian National Railways Act of 1919. In 1923, Grand Trunk was consolidated into the Canadian National Railway.

Ten short-line Grand Trunk railroads, mainly in Michigan, were consolidated by Canadian National into one US railroad, Grand Trunk Western Railroad, 9 May 1928.

Although the railroad today handles many different types of goods—grain, chemicals, lumber, paper—its most important customers are automobile manufacturers.

The Canadian National and Grand Trunk Western Routes

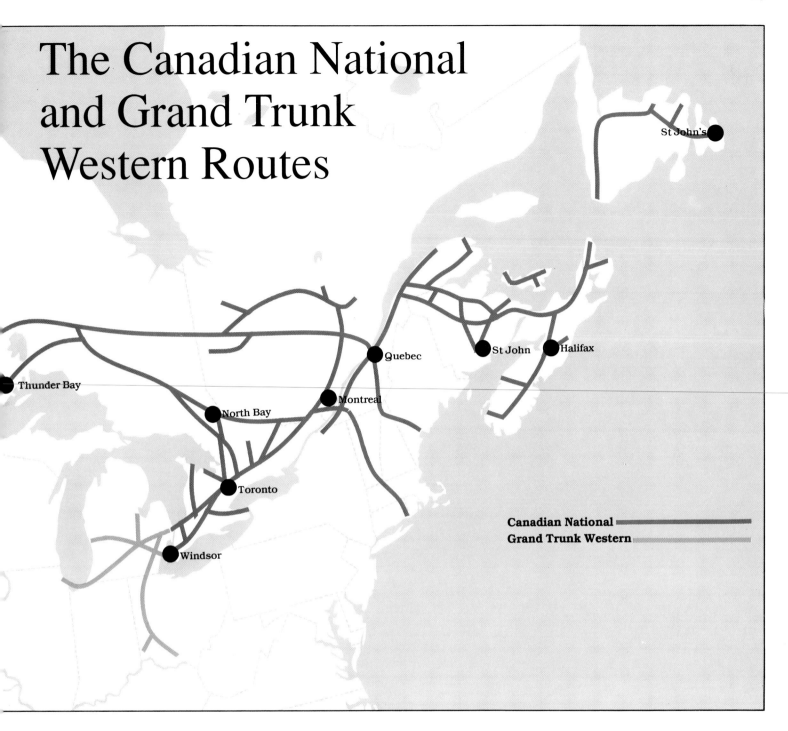

Thunder Bay

North Bay

Toronto

Windsor

Montreal

Quebec

St John

Halifax

St John's

Canadian National ▬▬▬▬▬
Grand Trunk Western ▬▬▬▬▬

Many thousands of tons of steel, plastics, and other raw materials travel to their huge plants each year. New cars and car parts are shipped by rail to car dealers all over North America and abroad. The railway's motto is 'Grand Trunk—the Good Track road.'

The Central Vermont Railway operates 375 miles of rail in the states of New York, New Hampshire, Massachusetts, Connecticut and the province of Quebec. In addition to serving shippers in its New England territory, it handles US—bound Canadian traffic from CN's eastern lines to the US rail system south of New England. It is headquartered in St Albans, Vermont.

The story of the CV goes back a long way. It was started by Vermont businessmen who needed a rail line to ship their goods to the rich markets of Montreal and New York City. The first few miles were built in 1848, only 12 years after Canada's first railway, the Champlain and St Lawrence, was opened to traffic.

Above: The Canadian/US trackage of the Canadian National and Grand Trunk Western rail systems. The CN operates some 22,520 miles of tracks with approximately 1830 locomotives of varying configurations, and approximately 80,690 various freight cars.

Canadian railwaymen first became involved in the CV in 1898, when the company needed more money and decided to allow the Grand Trunk to buy some of its shares. When Canadian National took over in 1923, it inherited that heavy interest in the CV. Nevertheless, the CV continued to operate officially as a separate company under its American owners.

Then, in 1927, disaster struck. Four days and nights of heavy rains and flooding wiped out almost one quarter of CV trackage. Bridges were washed away, ties and rails were twisted, broken, and scattered all over the countryside. Since the CV did not have enough money to make repairs, it looked as if the company would have to close down.

Compare the photo. *at left.* of a freight crossing the new International Railway Bridge near Niagra Falls with the vintage depiction on pages 24–25 of this text. Grand Trunk intermodal freight is shown here in some of its diversity—*at top:* piggyback truck trailers; *above:* tri-level enclosed auto trains, which, with tri-level auto parts trains, implement an important GT freight service.

It went into bankruptcy shortly afterwards, and Canadian National bought it at the subsequent auction.

Today, the CV provides CN with an important connection between Montreal and New York City. As well, it serves to link the New England towns along its route with major Canadian and American centers.

The Duluth, Winnepeg and Pacific Railway, headquartered in Wisconsin, has over 165 miles of track and handles US–bound Canadian traffic from CN's western lines to the US rail system south and east of Duluth and Superior.

Duluth, Winnipeg and Pacific is a rather strange name for this railroad. Although it originates in Duluth, Minnesota, and runs north to the Canadian border, it stops far short of Winnepeg, and never reaches the Pacific.

The original line was built in 1908 by local businessmen who wanted a fast, efficient way to ship lumber to the Great Lakes and the big cities in the midwestern states.

In 1902, William Mackenzie and Donald Mann of the Canadian Northern Railway completed their line from Lake Superior to Winnepeg. Because it ran very close to the Canada-United States border and a rail line between the two countries made good sense, Mackenzie and Mann decided to buy the DW&P and extend it south from Virginia to Duluth, and north to Fort Frances, Ontario, where it would link up with Canadian Northern.

Although the land was very rugged, the line was finished in 1912. The Canadian Northern now had access to two major ports on Lake Superior: what is now known as Thunder Bay, and Duluth.

When Canadian National took over the Canadian Northern, the Duluth, Winnepeg and Pacific came with it. Although it is not long, it is still an important railroad, providing a main link between Canada and the States.

It also has an impressive safety record. In 1986, SW&P employees achieved another outstanding year for work safety, with job-related accidents reduced by 30 percent from 1985. This qualified the railroad for the EH Harriman Memorial Silver Award for second place among Class II railroads, marking the third time in four years that DW&P earned the Silver Award, and following a Bronze Award in 1985.

CN's American railroads are important to both countries. Goods made in this country travel over their lines to reach the rich markets south of the border. And, too, their northbound trains carry many products needed by Canadians. It is a profitable exchange between good neighbours.

At right: A Central Vermont five-header freight passes through St Albans. *Above:* A Duluth, Winnipeg and Pacific Railway freight in Pokegama, Wisconsin. *Above right:* A train comprised, by mutual operating agreement, of CN, BN, GTW and DW&P rolling stock elements.

The People

CN is one of the largest employers in Canada. Special training is needed to do most jobs there. Many courses and apprentice programs are offered to help employees learn new skills. However, nearly all jobs require high school education, and quite a few are open only to university graduates.

Track is built and maintained by gangs of workers. The number of people in each gang can vary depending on the size and type of job to be done. Many of the workers in each gang are skilled in operating heavy machinery. Cranes, bulldozers, graders and a variety of special types of railway equipment must be handled safely and efficiently.

The engineering department is in charge of track work. This group also builds and looks after all railway bridges, tunnels and overpasses. Experienced professional engineers are needed to design and supervise the work.

Above: Grand Trunk yard workers fuel one of the line's 3000hp 16-cylinder diesels—it sure ain't the family van. *At left:* Cleanliness is part of most railroads' maintenance program—if they've taken time to clean it, they've probably taken time to fix it—and the engineers like to see the world outside. *Facing page:* This loco is taking on sand, to be released on the tracks ahead of its wheels for better traction if needed.

A freight train crew is usually made up of a conductor, an engineer and a brakeman. The conductor is a bit like the captain of a ship. He has to make sure that the train is on schedule and operates safely. The conductor knows the contents, weight and destination of all the cars on the train. If any cars or packages must be left at sidings or stations along the route, he supervises their delivery.

Before each trip, the conductor is given written train orders. These orders provide special instructions on train speeds and routes. The conductor must make sure that all members of his crew know what the train orders say and obey them.

The engineer drives the locomotive. He controls the train's speed using levers, air brakes and a throttle. The engineer must obey all train order instructions. On heavy traffic lines, signal lights along the track warn the engineer if another train is approaching. Sometimes he will have to pull the train into a siding to let a faster one pass. Before starting up again, the engineer waits for a signal from the conductor.

The engineer must be very alert at all times. If the train starts or stops too quickly, the contents of the cars could be damaged.

Many railroaders start their careers as brakemen. The brakeman does many different jobs, including uncoupling and coupling cars to make up a train, setting the brakes by turning the brake wheel on each car to make sure it does not move when it is stopped, and throwing switches so that the train takes the right track.

CN Rail moves passengers trains under contract with VIA Rail Canada and provides a conductor, a locomotive engineer and as many trainmen as are needed for the size of the train. On passenger trains, the brakemen are called trainmen and wear the same style of uniforms worn by the conductor. All other employees on the train, such as porters, in dayniters or sleeping cars, and stewards and waiters, in club cars, lounges and dining cars, work for VIA Rail Canada.

One of the most important and difficult jobs on the railway is that of train dispatcher. Although the dispatcher is not on board a freight train, the train cannot run without him. The dispatcher's job is almost like an air controller's job at an airport, except that it involves controlling train movements over railway lines rather than aircraft over flight paths.

There are two different types of track on the railway. Main line routes handle many trains each day. These lines are electronically wired so that signal lights and switches can be changed automatically. Dispatchers in charge of these main lines work from a large control board. The board shows where the trains are located as they pass through the dispatcher's territory. The dispatcher can change the signal lights and switches by remote control to guide the train on its route. As well, the dispatcher can talk by radio to the engineer.

Rail lines that handle less traffic do not have the costly electronic signal and switch systems. For trains running on these tracks, the dispatcher must make out detailed written train orders which the conductor and engineer follow very carefully. If the orders need to be changed, the dispatcher contacts the engineer by radio or sends a new set of train orders to the next station along the route. As the train passes the station, the station agent hands the orders to the locomotive engineer.

Night and day the railroad yards hum with activity; trains arrive and depart and thousands of cars are sorted onto the right tracks for the next leg of their journey.

Rather than working on trains, some locomotive engineers are assigned to operate yard switching engines. This work takes skill and experience. The engineer must back his locomotive gently up to a line of cars until the lead car couples with the locomotive. The cars are then hauled away onto another track where a train is being assembled for departure.

The locomotive engineer is helped in his job by yardmen. They stand by the cars as the locomotive backs up and guide the engineer with hand signals. Each time cars are move, the yardmen must release the hand brakes. When the cars arrive at their new location, the brakes are tightened again so that the car will not start rolling on its own. As well, the yardmen change the

switches so that the locomotive can move from one track to another.

From their control towers, yardmasters oversee all activity in the yard. They know where each car should be placed and help to direct the work of the switch crews. In some larger yards, the yardmaster electronically controls the switches so that each car rolls down a hump into the right track. As well, the yardmaster has remote control over special retarder brakes on the tracks. These brakes slow the cars down so that they roll at just the right speed to couple gently with the other cars on the track.

CN Rail's training programs and facilities are among the best in North America. And the locomotive and train simulator, located at CN Rail's transportation training center in western Canada, is symbolic of the railway's sophisticated, serious approach to training. Each year, about 1000 locomotive engineers, dispatchers, mechanics and supervisors complete courses under the guidance of a full-time staff of instructors.

For maintenance-of-way crews, CN Rail has established residential training centers where employees learn how to operate mechanized equipment safely and effectively. The equipment department also conducts a training program

The single line flowing motion of Canadian National's present logo *(above opposite)* reflects the efficient operations with which the line was and is kept vital, and replaced the old CN logo *(above)* in 1961. The CN's new 100-ton pressure tank hopper car design *(below)* and 100-ton box car *(below right)* design symbolize the CN's modernity.

for apprentices in those trades related to the maintenance, repair and manufacturing of railway rolling stock.

For managerial staff, CN Rail offers a wide range of courses conducted by a cadre of specialists skilled in training techniques.

A New Image

There came a day when the CNR was moving into the future so quickly that it felt it needed to streamline its corporate logo. The now familiar 'CN ' has been appearing in red, white, or blue since 1961, not only in Canada but around the world.

In April of 1959, Canadian National received the results of a comprehensive public attitude study based of field interviews with 4000 adult Canadians. This survey indicated that the public had a rather poor impression of CN and of the railway industry in general. Specifically, railways were regarded as being rather old-fashioned, slow to experiment with new ways of doing things and relatively unconcerned about improving their services to the public.

This study clearly showed that Canadian National was getting little public credit for its extensive modernization program. Why did the public still persist in looking upon the railway as unprogressive?

The company's public relations department decided that a large part of the answer could be summed up in the adage, 'Seeing is believing.' Canadian National had done a great deal to improve its plant, but most of the improvements were behind the scenes, largely hidden from public view. Little or nothing had been done to improve the package in which the product was sold. In its outward appearances—offices, equipment, signs, uniforms and graphics—the railway presented a drab Victorian façade, composed of countless unrelated and uncoordinated designs. What Canadian National needed was a fresh modern package to suit and do justice to its product.

There was little difficulty in deciding that what Canadian National needed was a comprehensive design program embracing every aspect of the face the company presented to the public. The objective was to develop a unified design approach aimed at giving CN a distinctive, easily recognizable identity and making it a stand-out in an increasingly complex and competitive business environment.

For these reasons, and taking into account the sort of image problem it faced, Canadian National ruled out the idea of a gradual transition and decided upon a bold and abrupt break with the past.

The Public Relations department engaged Jamas Valkus Inc of New York as a consultant to help CN organize a broad program of visual redesign, including a new corporate symbol. The task of creating the symbol itself was assigned to one of Canada's outstanding graphic designers, Allan Fleming of Toronto.

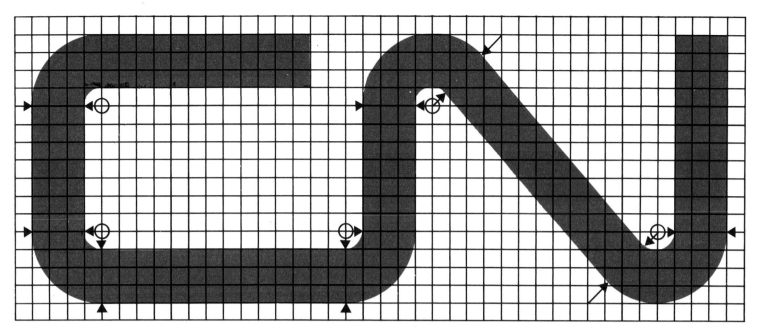

Early in 1960, the director of public relations presented the redesign proposals to the company's board of directors. The directors were unanimous and enthusiastic in their approval of the program. Then began the painstaking task of transforming the designs from a set of attractive and imaginative concepts into practical and economical realities.

The result was the now familiar symbol which spells out CN in one simple flowing line. It symbolized the one thing common to all of CN's principal activities: motion—the movement of men, materials and messages from one place to another.

Other elements in the massive face-lifting operation were to include standardized type styles, the systematic application of bright primary colours, careful attention to form and format; in short, a concern for excellence in design of everything that was to come before the public eye.

But by November it was becoming increasingly difficult to keep the lid on the story. About three weeks before the

publication date of the magazines, the Director of Public Relations received an urgent phone call from the Chief of Motive Power and Car Equipment. The latter explained that some 400 boxcars were almost ready to roll off the assembly line and that the manufacturer was asking for instructions as to how they should be painted. The cars were due to go into circulation as soon as the paint was dry.

To apply the newly approved boxcar design to this equipment order would mean that the new symbol would roll into public view—and perhaps be spotted by a newspaper photographer—in advance of the official announcement. Harris decided to take the risk, rather than have the old insignia applied to several hundred brand new cars.

It wasn't long before the lid was off. A few days before the internal publications were in the hands of employees, a photograph of one of the new boxcars appeared in a Montreal newspaper. The caption suggested that this was probably the first public glimpse of Canadian National's

Above: The tail end of this freight sports a caboose in a scene emblematic of the CN's industriousness amid the abundant beauty of its parent nation, Canada. *Right:* Another beauty shot—in this instance, a triple header boiling through the Redpass, Alberta area.

new trademark. It was. The press kit that was being held for later distribution was released immediately.

In other fields the design approach has had to be more durable. In working out exterior color schemes for passenger and freight trains, for example, the objective was to develop, document and distribute to all concerned a consistent design pattern that would be carefully followed for years to come.

The new paint schemes were applied on all rolling stock in accordance with normal maintenance schedules, as the locomotives and cars were shopped for their regular overhauls. New interior schemes for passenger cars have been worked out with the aim of creating a pleasant contemporary atmosphere while keeping the materials practical and durable. The old uniforms of the passenger train crews with their heavy navy-blue material and brass buttons are being replaced with lighter-weight cloth fashionably tailored in charcoal greys, bright blues and reds.

Certainly the redesign program has served to draw attention to the company in a dramatic way. Not everyone liked the new symbol when it first appeared, but at least a lot of people talked about it. Some described it as a bent paper clip, a tapeworm rampant, printed radio circuit, tortured snake and so on.

Happily, however, in this case familiarity didn't breed contempt. Acceptance of the new symbol, and some of the uses to which it began to be put, grew steadily from the outset.

The program has won a variety of major international awards for design excellence. A number of large companies, both in Canada and the United States, have come to CN for information and advice in the course of developing their own corporate identity programs.

With respect to the general public, a comprehensive study of attitudes conducted for CN by ORC International Ltd in 1966 confirmed that Canadian National had (since the 1959 findings) substantially improved its corporate image. Specifically, it had enhanced its reputation in terms of being 'progressive, efficiently run, trying to serve

Above left: This is the electronic train control console at Kamloops, BC, which directs freight movements between there and Jasper, Alberta. *Left:* A technician checks complex circuits at the CN Communications center in Toronto. *At top:* This Battle Creek area traffic control console serves the GTW's Chicago Division. *Above:* A technician attends a CN Communications microwave telephone service antenna.

the public well, providing job security and having good morale.'

In the seven years between the two surveys, the company had done many things to improve its plant and equipment, operating and sales methods and organizational structure. But certainly redesign was one of the key tools used in reflecting and communicating these other changes to the public.

It is the CN's belief that the new symbol stands as a visible mark of progress to remind people of the real and continuing improvements that are taking place behind the scenes in Canadian National, and that the whole visual redesign program is in fact helping to build and extend

the company's reputation for providing good service and merchandising it with modern marketing methods.

Computers and Telecommunications

Railways and computers were meant for each other. Since the CNR began using them in 1958, the company has adapted or developed specific systems to keep track of every piece of rolling stock, to operate switches and signals, and to test tracks and roadbeds. All these uses and many others were adopted in addition to normal business computerization of payroll, inventory control, customer records, and inter-office communication.

The use of modern-day electronics helps CN Rail achieve more efficiency in its operations and today the railway is one of the largest business users of computers in North America.

CN Rail's computer-based information system is one of the most advanced of any railway in the world. Called TRACS, for Traffic Reporting And Control System, it feeds information to central data banks over 299,460 miles of communications circuits.

To complement the TRACS system, CN Rail developed the Yard Inventory System. This computerized system provides yard personnel with the information they need to quickly sort incoming traffic and reassign it according to destination.

Of course, computer applications go beyond actual train movements and CN Rail today relies on computers in just about every branch of service from purchasing to employee record keeping.

Every time a Canadian makes a train or airline reservation, reads an out-of-town story in a local newspaper, listens to a weather forecast or transfers money through a bank, the information he received probably travelled over the CNCP network. CNCP was established as an independent and equal partnership between two owners—CN and Canadian Pacific Ltd.

CNCP introduced the first network designed especially for computers in 1967. It was an analog service called Broadband Exchange Service, and could also handle voice. With the development of more efficient digital technology, CNCP introduced its Infodat service for private dedicated lines in 1974.

Two years later with the development of packet switching—a method by which traffic is broken into small 'packages' for transmission across a network—CNCP introduced its Infoswitch network.

Now CNCP is preparing for the office of the future with Infotex, a new service introduced in 1981.

With the increasing use of personal computers, much of the information now handled in the form of words or figures on paper in offices will instead be generated, edited, transmitted, stored and recalled in the form of electronic signals. Infotex will make possible such services as communicating word processors, electronic mail, electronic filing systems and 'in' baskets from which executives will be able to retrieve their messages on TV-like screens at their desks, at home or with portable units while travelling.

CNCP is also involved in satellite communications and is developing, with the department of communications, new techniques for moving voice, data and video signals via Canada's Anik satellites. Trials have been carried out with fiber optics—glass fibers which can transmit signals

as a beam of light—to test their capabilities when laid along railway rights-of-way.

Canadian National, like several other railways, has been involved in telecommunications since its earliest days.

As railways were built across Canada, telegraph lines were strung along poles placed on the right-of-way. Primarily used to endure safe and efficient train operation, the lines also carried inter-office messages for the company. Service to the public took two forms—people could send messages in the form of telegrams and large companies could lease lines exclusively for their messages.

CN Communications today includes NorthwesTel, Terra Nova Telecommunications, CNCP Telecommunications and Telecommunications Terminal Systems. Besides being part of an integrated national network, each division has its separate use.

Through NortwesTel and Terra Nova Tel, CN provides telephone services in two of the remotest parts of Canada, the northwest including Yukon, the western Northwest Territories and northern British Columbia and rural Newfoundland, an area which includes isolated fishing communities around the coast and on off-shore islands.

In northwestern Canada, CN was given the responsibility of operating, on a commercial basis, telephone facilities which had previously been provided directly by government or military authorities.

CN took over limited facilities and invested in modern equipment to provide the latest in telephone service to such places as Inuvik, Tuktoyaktuk and Old Crow, as well as the two territorial capitals, Whitehorse and Yellowknife.

NorthwesTel, CN's northern operation has one of the most challenging jobs of any telephone company, serving an area of 14,570,000 square miles with a population of less than 70,000. Yet its digital switching equipment is among the most up-to-date in the world.

NorthwesTel is now a CN Communications arm in British Columbia, the Yukon, and the Northwest Territories. It has been expanding into the more remote reaches of these areas, and in 1985 it installed satellite communication ground stations to improve service to five communities—Pelly Bay, Spence Bay, Gjoa Haven, Fort Franklin and Telegraph Creek.

In Newfoundland, CN was made responsible for the telephone and telegraph services of the former department of posts and telegraphs following that province's entry into Confederation in 1949. Terra Nova Tel, as CN's Newfoundland telephone company is called, provides telephone service to the entire island of Newfoundland with the exception of the urbanized areas in the Avalon and Burin peninsulas, and around Corner Brook and Grand Falls. It provides telegraph and other specialized telecommunications services for the entire province.

Terra Nova Tel is the local telephone company in such coastal outports as Joe Batt's Arm and St Anthony, as well as to many of the off-shore islands. Its headquarters are in Gander, the largest urban community served.

Terra Nova Tel built the first microwave link across the island, and has an extensive network of submarine cables

to serve outports and off-shore islands. Maintaining telephone service in these rugged conditions is a challenge, and again CN has turned to solid-state and digital technology to provide reliable services.

CNCP Telecommunications is the only coast-to-coast telecommunications carrier in Canada operated under a unified management structure. Backbone of CNCP services is a coast-to-coast microwave network which carries voice, data, facsimile, broadcasting and other electronic signals.

CNCP introduced Telex service into North America in 1956, but the first recorded long-distance transmission of computer data took place over the CNCP network between Saskatoon and Toronto in 1955. Since that time CNCP has move ahead to adapt new telecommunications technology to the task of providing up-to-date service for business, industry and government departments.

Telecommunications Terminal Systems was launched in 1982 as a partnership with Canadian Pacific Limited. It deals with communications equipment. A recent venture was the launching of TTS into the large office automation equipment market during 1984.

With all its emphasis on computers and telecommunications, it is interesting that CN Communications was not

the CN division to build a structure that has been a great help to communications. It was the CN Hotels that built the CN Tower in Toronto.

The CN Tower

When the CN Tower project was first announced, it seemed almost impossible. At the time, Toronto was reeling from the effects of a major building boom, which had dotted its skyline with monolith buildings. The highest soared a staggering 750 feet. Now CN boasted that it would build a structure more than twice that height—possibly as high as the world-leading Ostankino Tower in Moscow, maybe even higher. Toronto's ascending skyline had introduced a problem for existing communications systems. Pre-skyscraper transmission towers were simply not high enough to broadcast over the new obstacles. As a result, signal-bounce, or ghosting, was becoming increasingly severe.

Fortunately, the Tower designers had the foresight to realize that the new buildings were only the beginning. In the future, they predicted downtown buildings would grow to 1000 feet and more. As a result, the proportions for the Tower were set, with its microwave receivers at 1100 feet and its antenna topping off at the 1815 feet mark.

Its location, at the front door of the city, also determined the need for the Tower to be more than a communications structure. It would have to be attractive. In addition, as an integral part of the populated downtown landscape, the incorporation of public facilities was assumed from the onset.

While several individuals figured prominently, no one person can be given the credit for the total design and construction of the Tower. From the initial proposal in 1968, to the final model in 1972 and eventually the Tower itself, which was completed in 1976, the project involved a consortium of experts from around the world. Initially, the plan called for three towers linked with structural bridges. Prohibited by construction and financial limitations, the design gradually evolved into a single Tower.

Because it is the first of its size and type, the CN Tower broke new ground in many of its answers to engineering challenges. No one had ever built a structure which would rise as high off the ground. Consequently, never had a foundation been devised which would bore so deeply into the ground. This in itself represented many engineering breakthroughs. First, beginning in 1972, an elaborate soil testing operation was put into effect to assess the condition of the bedrock and its reaction to changes in hydrostatic pressure. Equipped with this information, the

Above: Inside the CN Tower's 'Sparkles' nightclub. *At right:* The CN Tower is the apex, so to speak, of a downtown Toronto CN complex. At the base of the Tower can be seen the CN Convention Center, and CN Hotels' semi-circular L'Hôtel. The Tower's microwave equipment is housed in the 'doughnut' collar under its rotunda, which is below the Tower's long needle antenna.

designers developed foundation specifics which would assure the Tower's stability. On 6 February 1973, construction crews moved in. Over 62,000 tons of earth and shale were removed by giant backhoes, digging 50 feet into the ground. Next, the 22-foot thick concrete and steel foundation was erected on a base of hand- and machine-smoothed shale. When finished, the Y-shaped foundation contained 9200 cubic yards of concrete, 500 tons of reinforcing steel and 40 tons of thick, tensioning cable.

Barely four months after construction began, all was in readiness for the above-ground operation. First, 12 steel and wood brackets, weighing 350 tons had to be systematically lifted, inch by inch, up the sides of the Tower. The task required 45 hydraulic jacks and miles of steel cable. Once in place, one-fifth of a mile above the ground, workmen bolted the brackets to tensioned steel bars and placed concrete in the wooden frames. Next, a three-foot high concrete compression ring was placed around the outside edge of the brackets to make one strong unit.

Twenty-four hours a day, five days a week, concrete was poured into a massive mold or 'slipform.' As the concrete hardened, the 'slipform,' supported by a ring of climbing jacks that were powered by hydraulic pressure, moved upwards, gradually decreasing in size to produce the gracefully tapered contour. To assure its strength and quality, the concrete was mixed on the site, continuously checked and tested, then reinforced with a unique system of post-tensioning which produced a strength of 6000 pounds per square inch. The legs of the Tower are hollow, as is its hexagonal core which houses all of the electrical cables and water piping. The concrete portion of the Tower was completed in February 1974. Situated at the top of the concrete is the 'World's Highest Public Observation Gallery,' the Space Deck. All that extends above it is the 335 foot steel antenna. A two-story structure, the Space Deck was created by cantilevering a concrete platform around the top edge of the Tower. Next, from the overhang of its roof, a glass wall was suspended, banking inwards at the bottom and completely enclosing the upper story in glass. An enclosed elevator transports visitors to the glass-surrounded viewing balcony. In August 1974, work began on the seven-story Skypod which would ultimately house two observation decks.

Intrinsic to the construction of the CN Tower was the mighty crane, which over its four years of round-the-clock service lifted some 50,000 tons of material and machinery. With the completion of the Skypod, however, its usefulness also ended. Fortunately, the answer to dismantling the crane and erecting the enormous antenna came in one solution—'Olga', a giant Sikorsky helicopter. Reduced to eight sections, the crane was brought swiftly down to earth and the 39 pieces of the antenna (the heaviest weighing eight tons) were lifted into place with remarkable precision.

For many, the purpose behind the familiar donut-shaped collar at the base of the Skypod is a mystery. Technically, it is known as a radome and without its protection, the sensitive microwave dishes which receive the transmissions would be ravaged by the elements. Made of teflon-coated, fiberglass-rayon fabric, it is strong enough to hold the weight of an average adult male, yet measures a mere one-thirty-second of an inch thick. Its balloon-like shape is the result of inflating the skin to five times its normal size then maintaining constant air pressure. A second radome protects the full length of the antenna. Designed to prevent ice buildup, it's made of 11/2-inch thick glass-reinforced plastic.

In September 1973, the Tower became the tallest structure in Toronto and by January 1974, it was unrivalled in Canada. The top of the 'slipform' concrete, 1464 feet, was reached on 22 February 1974 and to that was added a special 16-foot concrete extension which would serve as a base for the transmission mast. With the placing of the 36th piece of the antenna mast, at 9:52 am on 31 March 1975, the CN Tower surpassed Moscow's Ostankino Tower to become the 'World's Tallest Freestanding Structure.' On hand to record the milestone was Ross McWhirter, then editor of the *Guinness Book of World Records*, of London, England.

During the Dedication Ceremony on 1 October 1976, presided over by Prime Minister Pierre E Trudeau, a time capsule was placed in the wall on the Indoor Observation Deck. It will be opened on 1 October 2076. Only 17

other self-supporting structures in world history have held the title tallest. At 1815 feet 5 inches, the CN Tower brought the title to Canada for the first time.

The tower has been the site of many height-related records. As a promotion for the Egg Marketing Board, Patrick Ballie, 17, of Toronto, beat the *Guinness Book* record for egg dropping by over 500 feet. He dropped a Grade A egg, unscathed, from 1120 feet into a specially-designed net, on 27 July 1979. The first person to parachute off the Tower was a member of the construction crew, Bill Eustace, aka 'Sweet William', on 9 November 1975: for his daring, he was discharged. Hollywood stuntman, Dar Robinson, made two jumps from the Level 5 of the Skypod. The first was made with a parachute on 21 September 1979, while shooting a scene for the movie 'Highpoint.' The second, which was conducted for the television show 'That's Incredible,' involved only wire cables to break the fall. To mark the Tower's fourth birthday, two mountain climbers, David Smart, 17, and Gerald Banting, 30, attempted an unauthorized climb up the outside of the Tower on 23 June 1980. They made it halfway before backing down. Once a year, the Tower's staircase are opened to the public, to raise funds for the United Way. As a rule, this is an autumn event, with climbers starting their ascent just above the main lobby and concluding at the Skypod. Many records have been set and broken at this event.

Not only is the CN Tower the tallest freestanding structure in the world but it is also probably the safest. Everything from the forces of nature to man-made disasters were considered in the formulation of its design.

The upper reaches of the Tower are continually bombarded by turbulent winds. To test the Tower's design against this and other extreme wind forces, a special 'wind tunnel,' the first of its kind in North America, was created at the University of Western Ontario. Within the tunnel, construction models of the Tower were tested under conditions which simulated the maximum wind strength based on the analysis of a 1000-year time frame. The wind speed reached in the tunnel measured 130 mph.

When plans for the Tower were concluded, their wind resistance factor was established at 260 mph. In addition to the structure, the windows of the Tower, which are armor-plated, were carefully designed for extreme wind tolerance. The outside panes are three-eighths of an inch thick and the inside panes are one fourth of an inch thick. They can withstand internal or external pressure in excess of 120 pounds per square inch. The ability of the CN Tower to wobble under extreme wind conditions was not overlooked either. Two 10-ton swinging counterweights, mounted on the antenna, ensure that the intentional sway of the Tower never exceeds acceptable levels. There's certainly not a more exceptional or perhaps safer place in the city from which to view the awesome spectacle of a raging thunderstorm.

Though the tower is struck by lightning about 60 times a year, there is never any danger. Every surface which could possibly attract lightning is attached to three copper

Despite the Tower's extreme height *(at left)*, it is within 1.1 inches of absolute plumb—ie, perfectly vertical. One danger designed against in the Tower's construction was 'torsional oscillation'—the tendency of tall structures to twist with the rotational motion of the Earth, just as water twists down a sink drain. Such 'twisting,' if unprepared for, would no doubt cause a catastrophe.

Below right: A view of the Tower from behind L'Hôtel, in downtown Toronto. *Opposite:* CN Hotels' period-style Hotel Vancouver offers its 500 luxurious rooms amid the exquisite natural splendor of British Columbia's queen city. Complete facilities include meeting and board rooms, sumptuous restaurants and bars, and complete health and fitness facilities. *Above:* CN's elegant Château Laurier, which overlooks the Ottawa River, in Ottawa.

strips running down the Tower, connected to 42 22-foot grounding rods buried 20 feet below the surface.

To ensure against the possibility of ice or snow building up and falling to earth, every place where ice is likely to collect (such as changes in the roof contour) is ice-proofed, either with de-icing tracers or sheathed with a cling-proof plaster surface.

Fire prevention has always been a Tower priority. Smoking is not permitted on most of the public areas. All of the construction materials used were either fire-proof or fire resistant. Even the interior furnishings selected are as fireproof as possible. In the unlikely event of fire, emergency generators, located in the basement, are capable of supplying power for the elevators and other systems, including the emergency fire pumps which can pump water to the top of the Tower at a rate of 500 gallons a minute. A reservoir of water is also maintained in the Skypod itself.

Since its opening, the Tower has boasted a perfect record thanks to its carefully conceived design, interior monitoring system, and diligent security force.

Next to the Tower itself, the 'Universal Man,' a 10-foot high by 18-foot wide bronze sculpture, is one of the popular CN Tower subjects for photographers. Created by Canadian artist Gerald Gladstone, it is one of the

Above: The impeccable elegance of Zoé's Cafe—part of the luxurious accomodations of CN Hotels' Château Laurier. Château Laurier has served kings. queens and heads of state from all over the world since 1912. The elegance which is also evident in Château Laurier's French baroque Grand Ballroom *(above right)* and classically-appointed Reading Room *(lower right)* continues a tradition that began when the CN determined to build not merely adequate. but some of the finest, passenger accomodations in the world. Equally elegant. but in a different style. is the CNH Hotel Newfoundland's Cabot Club Restaurant *(below).* in St John's. CN Hotels comprises 10 excellently-appointed hotels nationwide. with full service at each.

largest bronze castings ever made and was air-freighted from the Singer Foundry in England in nine sections.

In addition to this impressive artwork (which signifies earthbound human energies reaching towards a higher knowledge through communications), the outdoor plaza also features a mounted 1000-pound piece of the great Matterhorn mountain, which was presented to the Tower in April 1981 in conjunction with the Salute to Switzerland exhibition.

Today, both public and experts from the field of construction come to marvel at the Tower which stands as a testament to human ingenuity and achievement.

Its official owner is CN Tower Limited, a subsidiary of Canadian National and part of the CN Hotels, but few will argue when one says it really belongs to Canada. While some day, some place, someone might build a Tower higher, the significance of the CN structure and its tremendous contributions will never be diminished.

CN Hotels

It may seem a little odd today that a transportation company should own a chain of hotels and the world's tallest self-supporting structure. Years ago, when all railways operated passenger trains, they needed to set up lodgings for travellers.

Thus railway companies such as Grand Trunk, Grand Trunk Pacific, Canadian Northern and Intercolonial, built large, elegant hotels in cities across Canada.

When CN was formed to take over these early railway companies, it naturally inherited their hotels. Many of them remain impressive landmarks, such as the Chateau Laurier in Ottawa, or beautiful, rustic Jasper Park Lodge.

CN's Jasper Park Lodge dates back to 1922, when its first building was constructed on the shore of Lac Beauvert. With the majestic Canadian Rockies rising above it *(above opposite)*. Jasper Park Lodge is ideal for those with a taste for not only spectacular scenery but also such genteel comforts as Point Cabin (which interior is shown *above*) and room service via bicycle *(below opposite)*. Actually, Jasper Park Lodge is 'fit for everyone.'

This CN hotel, nestled deep in the Canadian Rockies, was visited by plain, every-day Canadians as well as kings, queens and Movie stars. The central lodge building was burned to the ground in 1952, but it was rebuilt and the hotel is still an active, luxurious resort.

Today, CN's chain extends from Vancouver to St John's. The older hotels have kept their charming architecture on the outside, but the interiors have been completely redone. The interior redesign has included modern bedrooms, convention facilities, discotheques and fine restaurants.

CN hotels are important to the cities in which they are located because they provide hundreds of jobs for local people. As well, they attract tourists and large convention groups to the area. The money these visitors spend during their stay helps to support stores, restaurants, night clubs and many other businesses.

Since the first hotels were built to serve the railway's needs, lifestyles have changed. Today, CN hotel guests arrive by plane, bus and car, as well as by train.

CN Hotels have kept up every step of the way, but have not lost their historical presence. The Chateau Laurier underwent a renovation in the early 1980s to prepare for its 75th birthday in 1987, but lost none of its historical charm. CN Hotels has reclaimed management of the Queen Elizabeth and Vancouver Hotels from the Hilton organization, previously hired to manage them. These hotels underwent renovations similar to the Chateau Laurier's, all as part of a five-year program instituted in the early 1980s aimed at integrating all CN Hotel properties into one unified chain of first-class hotels.

CN On the Road

CN has its own large trucking fleets, from tractor-trailers to smaller city delivery trucks. By far the most noticed of the CN fleet was the CNX truck which moved on city streets delivering and picking up shipments.

CNX used large tractor-trailers to move goods between cities and then transfer the load to smaller trucks. The express division installed one of the most modern computerized shipment-tracing systems in North America. The system checks the incoming shipment, produces bills for the customers and keeps track as the shipment moves across Canada. In addition, it uses the knowledge stored in its computer to do the accounting for the division.

In 1983 the Board of Directors of CN gave authority to consolidate the administration of Express (CNX) and Trucking (CNTL) services in order to create one competitive highway-based unit providing trucking and related distribution services.

The new unit, then known as CNX/CN Trucking, began the difficult task of forming a single management team to direct the activities of a lean and efficient organization. By mid-1984 the single management team was working well and financial savings and new business opportunities resulting from the integration were becoming apparent. In order to capitalize on these advances a strong promotional program was developed, beginning with a change of name for the organization—to CN Route.

During 1984, compatible accounting and management information systems for the two divisions were established, and offices, terminals and maintenance facilities were rationalized. Following a hearing and a vote conducted by the Canadian Labour Relations Board, the terminal and fleet operations of the two divisions were integrated, providing customers with a single pick-up and delivery service.

Above: In one of CN's intermodal freight yards, a piggyback container-trailer is positioned to be loaded on a flatcar. *Above right:* This CN Route trucker climbs into the cab of his big White Freightliner in Alberta—in preparation for the run west *(below right)* to Vancouver. Note the new CN Route logo on both tractor cab and trailer. Such diversified service greatly benefits the CN's customers.

CN Route, which now operates 53 terminals across the country, faces a difficult task complicated by increasing competition in its field of activity and by the effects of deregulation on the trucking industry. The new unit has, however, made a good beginning and has good prospects not only for survival but for substantial development in the years ahead.

CN's role in truck transportation does not stop there. CN owns separate trucking companies which have kept their own names and operate independently. Two other CN trucking companies are Husband Transport and Midland Superior Express. Husband operates mostly in Ontario and Quebec and Midland Superior has its head office in Calgary, but its trucks carry goods to many different cities across the country. Husband Transport (Quebec), in a joint arrangement with the government of Quebec, acquired the trucking interests of Les Enterprises Bussieres, giving it coast-to-coast trucking connections.

Much of the trucking companies' business comes from combined road-rail operations. Many business firms and factories are not big enough to have a rail line built to their plant. They depend on trucking companies, such as the ones CN owns, to deliver goods.

The modern method of transportation is not to have trucking companies and the railway competing against each other. Instead the advantages of the trucks for short distances and the railways for long distances are combined.

Cement, meat, chemicals, paper, tobacco, electrical appliances and household furnishings are just a few of the many products CN's trucking companies carry.

Above: The freighter Georges Alexander Lebel, in the days of CN Marine (note markings). On its way to Alaska, this Aquatrain *(above right)* shows yet another aspect of CN intermodality—however, CN is selling its Crown corporations. *Below right:* The Marine Atlantic ferry *Bluenose.*

CN Goes to Sea

People in Canada's east coast have always used the sea for transportation. When Newfoundland joined Confederation in 1949, the CNR was asked to take over its rail lines. At the same time, the company began operating the ferries which ran between the mainland and the new island Province.

Despite highway and rail links between Maritime cities, water transportation is important to the region. CN Marine operated ships in four Atlantic provincial areas. CN Marine became a Crown corporation in September of 1986, and in keeping with CN Rail's future plans, was sold to Marine Atlantic, Incorporated, which is itself owned by a Crown corporation.

Still the CN Marine story is an interesting facet of CN's overall history. For instance, Prince Edward Island and Newfoundland are both separated from mainland Canada by water, and need fast, reliable ferries to the mainland.

The ferry service joining Newfoundland to Nova Scotia runs from North Sydney on Cape Breton Island to two terminals, Port aux Basques on the southwestern tip of Newfoundland winter and summer, and Argentia further up the coast near St John's during the summer. The North Sydney-Argentia trip is a long one. It takes 18 hours to travel the 264 miles across the Cabot Strait.

The distance between Prince Edward Island and its closest neighbor, New Brunswick, is much shorter. The crossing from Borden to Cape Tormentine can be made in 45 minutes.

Each year, millions of tons of freight are carried. Ships leaving the island provinces take farm produce, raw materials and manufactured goods to markets on the mainland. On the return trip, they bring products from the rest of Canada and the world to the people of Newfoundland and Prince Edward Island.

CN Marine operated a year-round ferry service between Yarmouth, and Portland, Maine. This route is still a truck-oriented shortcut for freight travelling on the *Marine Evangeline* between southern Nova Scotia and the New England states.

In addition, thousands of tourists from the United States use the ferry *Bluenose* to visit Canada for a holiday. The service is now offered during the summer months between Yarmouth and Bar Harbor, Maine by Marine Atlantic.

One of the busiest routes in the service is the Saint John-Digby connection that operates year-round. The *Princess of Acadia* plies the 141–mile crossing every day, carrying commercial traffic and thousands of tourists in the summer, between New Brunswick and Nova Scotia.

Dinner and dance mini-cruises help attract many of the 240,000 people who travel aboard the *Acadia* annually. And its value as a shortcut for freight is pointed up in the fact it carries more than 25,000 trucks and tractor trailers each year.

A key feature of the *Acadia* is that it can handle drop trailers. Trucking firms using the CN service drop their trailers at the two terminals where CN Marine personnel picked them up, drove them aboard, and locked them

These pages: Note the Marine Atlantic logo on the stack of this sleek ferry, the *Princess of Acadia,* which plies the Maritime waterways daily, carrying commercial and passenger traffic between New Brunswick and Nova Scotia—a much needed service for the inhabitants of the Maritime provinces.

down to the ship's deck. This saved trucking companies from tying up their tractors for extended periods of time.

Along the rugged coastlines of Newfoundland and Labrador are some of the most isolated communities in Canada. The land is rocky and windswept. No roads come within 500 or 1000 miles of these outports. The people make their living from the sea, as their families have done for generations before them. In winter, some are locked on shore by the ice.

Radio communications and the ships in the coastal service are their only contact with the outside world. The ships are their lifeline, bringing much-needed supplies and help in times of emergency.

The captains and crews of the coastal ships are highly skilled. They must weave a path through narrow channels, past rocky shoals and in and out of tiny harbors.

Life in an outport is lonely and hard. But people who live there do not wish to leave. The men and ships that served CN Marine's coastal service and who now serve Marine Atlantic, Inc. are helping to preserve the outport's way of life.

To handle the heavy volume of people and goods, Marine Atlantic's ships are built to handle different types of traffic, such as freight cars, large transport trucks, containers, trailers and automobiles. Some ferries also have ice-breaking capabilities with extra-thick hulls and powerful engines to force their way through ice jams that block the routes in wintertime.

CN Marine achievements included construction of a new ship, the *Caribou*, for Newfoundland service; par-

Above: The $180,000,000 convention center complex Metro Toronto, the largest of its kind in Canada, is a CN Real Estate project. In Newfoundland, Terra Transport freight transportation *(above right)* and Terra Transport interurban buses keep things, and people, moving.

ticipation by the Gulf ferry *Ambrose Shea* in the start of the 1984 Tall Ships trans-Atlantic race; and acquisition of computer-aided design and drafting terminals to increase the skills and productivity of engineering personnel.

CN Real Estate

When the railways were built, Canadian communities were much smaller than they are now. In fact, many cities in western Canada were not founded until after the rail lines came through to open up the country. In those early days, railway stations and yards were the center of activity. Factories, offices, shops and houses grew up around them.

As those centers grew larger and became cities, houses and industries spread further into the countryside. Over the years, many Canadian communities have become large, bustling cities. Immigrants from around the world have come to live in places such as Halifax, Montreal, Toronto, Winnipeg, Edmonton and Vancouver.

At the same time, land in the center of those cities, where the railways first located their yards and buildings, has become extremely valuable.

In the early 1960s, CN began to look for new ways to make better use of this valuable downtown property. Many factories and industries had moved away from Canadian city centers. In the suburbs, land was cheaper

and there was more room to expand. Large numbers of freight tracks were no longer needed right in the middle of the city. Too, some railway buildings and yards in downtown areas were old and out-of-date. The time was ripe for a new beginning.

Montreal was the first city where new development took place on CN land. By 1962, an entire new city block, called Place Ville Marie, had been created. A beautiful, 45-story office tower stands in the center. It is surrounded by an outdoor plaza. Beneath the plaza, hundreds of stores form a colorful shopping mall.

The building of Place Ville Marie was just the start of things to come. Montreal now has five kilometres of connecting indoor passageways lined with shops. Montrealers can reach two hotels, 36 restaurants, four movie theatres, 4000 parking spaces, two railway stations, 10 office buildings, a huge exhibition hall and a subway station without going outdoors. It is a city within a city, and most of it on CN land.

CN, the developers, and city planners thus work together to decide how the land can best be used.

Since Place Ville Marie was built, CN has been involved in other similar projects. In Saskatoon, the railway moved its tracks and yards to the outskirts of the city. This made room for Midtown Plaza, a complex which includes shopping areas, a 12-story office building, a convention center and a community theatre.

CN has also helped to rebuild large areas of downtown Moncton. A new CN hotel, city hall and shopping center are just part of new complexes in the New Brunswick city.

CN Real Estate achieved a notable development and construction feat in 1984 with the completion, on time and on budget, of the $180 million Metro Toronto Convention Centre Complex—the largest facility of its kind in Canada. Occupying seven square miles along Toronto's Front Street West and adjacent to the CN Tower the project was initiated and carried through by CN Real Estate as part of its mandate to develop the maximum commercial potential of CN holdings across Canada. Officially opened by Queen Elizabeth II in October 1984, the project has won recognition for CN Real Estate as an important presence in the development and construction field in Canada.

TerraTransport

TerraTransport provides rail and highway freight transportation and inter-urban bus passenger services in Newfoundland. It has recently undergone a five-year revitalization program, completed in 1985, modernizing its operations. However, despite the importance of the services it provides, TerraTransport has been losing money steadily in the past few years.

The Canadian government, which funded the revitalization program, is now evaluating the costs and benefits of TerraTransport in the context of overall Newfoundland transportation needs. This evaluation will determine the future of TerraTransport, and CN is looking for a solution that will relieve it of the current financial burden while still providing Newfoundland with efficient and economical freight transportation services.

Looking Ahead

Growth can only occur where there is a willingness to change. For a company, that means adapting to the reality of the needs of its customers and owners, and of the business environment in which it operates.

When a few Montrealers established British North America's first railway a century and a half ago, they could not possibly have imagined that their efforts would lead to the remarkable company Canadians own today.

The future of CN is not entirely certain—many of its divisions are Crown corporations, of which some are cur-rently being sold off. However, in one form or another, CN and its many services can look forward to being around for a good long time.

Canadian National and Canada have come a long way together.

Below: CN Rail freight traffic on the move in Saint John, New Brunswick. With such special services as Dimensional Load Shipment for extra large loads (see the cylindrical items that the train on photo right, here, is carrying), and with such powerful, mechanically sophisticated modern road switchers as those in the yard shown *at right,* CN Rail is indeed ready for the future. Changes are in store, however—as always, in the history of a great railroad.

Index